NO-GIMMICK GUIDE TO MANAGING STRESS

NO-GIMMICK GUIDE TO MANAGING STRESS
Effective options for every lifestyle

E. Joseph Neidhardt, M.D.
Malcolm S. Weinstein, Ph.D.
Robert F. Conry, Ph.D.

Cartoons by Janette Lush

Self-Counsel Press Inc.
a subsidiary of
International Self-Counsel Press Ltd.
Canada U.S.A.
(Printed in Canada)

First edition: December, 1985

Second edition: October, 1990; Reprinted: September, 1991

Canadian Cataloging in Publication Data
    Neidhardt, E.J.
    No-gimmick guide to managing stress

    (Self-counsel psychology series)
    Previously published as: Managing stress: a complete self-help guide.
    ISBN 0-88908-886-1

    1. Stress management. I. Weinstein, Malcolm S., 1942 - II. Conry, Robert F.
III. Title. IV. Title: Managing stress. V. Series.
BF575.S75N44 1990   155.9'042   C90-091307-X

Cover photo by Wallace Garrison/Image Finders, Vancouver

Self-Counsel Press Inc.
a subsidiary of
International Self-Counsel Press Ltd.
Head and Editorial Office
1481 Charlotte Road
North Vancouver, British Columbia V7J 1H1

U.S. Address
1704 N. State Street
Bellingham, Washington 98225

CONTENTS

LIST OF SAMPLES

LIST OF TABLES

ACKNOWLEDGMENTS

In preparing these stress management programs, we have relied extensively on previously published materials, and we would like to acknowledge our great debt to the pioneering work of researchers such as Walter Cannon, Johannes H. Schultz, Hans Selye, and Edmund Jacobson. We also express our sincere appreciation for help in many forms, generously given by our Advisory Committee: Frederic Bass, M.D., D.Sc. (Vancouver, British Columbia); Herbert Benson, M.D. (Boston, Massachusetts); Gerald Bonham, M.D. (Calgary, Alberta); Josephine Flaherty, Ph.D. (Ottawa, Ontario); Peter R. Grantham, M.D. (Vancouver, British Columbia); Suzanne Haynes, Ph.D. (Chapel Hill, North Carolina); Wolfgang Luthe, M.D. (North Vancouver, British Columbia); Chandra H. Patel, M.D. (Surrey, England); Kenneth R. Pelletier, Ph.D. (Berkeley, California); Gerald D. Pulvermacher, Ph.D. (Ottawa, Ontario); Gerald M. Rosen, Ph.D. (Seattle, Washington); Margo Sanderson, M.A. (Vancouver, British Columbia); Carl Thoresen, Ph.D. (Stanford, California); and Ronald G. White, Ph.D. (Sydney, Australia).

While this Advisory Committee contributed in various ways and in varying degrees to the content of these programs, they are in no way responsible for the final product. We assume full responsibility for the programs and the ideas presented in this book.

Out of clutter, find simplicity.
From discord, make harmony.
In the middle of difficulty lies opportunity.

—Albert Einstein

INTRODUCTION

Stress-related disorders have become increasingly common in Western society, and the wear and tear caused by chronic stress can contribute to physical and mental breakdown. Some disorders, such as hypertension, have reached almost epidemic proportions. Because of these increases, stress and ways of dealing with it are a major target of medical and psychological researchers.

Of course, we must not go too far in attributing all disease to stress. A person's health is, after all, the result of complex environmental, biological, behavioral, and health care factors. Regardless of the origins of disease and health, stress deserves our attention in the treatment of disease and in the promotion of health.

This book brings together in one volume a seven-part series of modules that were developed by the Western Center for Preventive and Behavioral Medicine with the support of the Health Promotion Directorate, Health and Welfare Canada. Six stress management programs were developed for the modules, and all were systematically evaluated through practical use by clinicians and their patients and clients. More than 50 physicians, community health nurses, social workers, and psychologists participated in the development of these programs.

The programs are —

- Personal planning skills
- Progressive relaxation training
- Quieting
- Autogenic methods
- Communication skills
- General health and well-being

Each program can be used independently — you may find one or two of them in combination particularly attractive to your lifestyle — or all the programs can be used as parts of a total stress management program.

You will find helpful evaluation and stress-assessment work sheets throughout the book to help you set your stress management goals. Progress charts to help you attain those goals and measure your progress are included in the appendix.

The aim of each program is to help people manage their own stress problems, and to help them become less dependent on expensive drugs and clinical services. In fact, effective stress management produces benefits far beyond symptom relief. It actually releases energy and increases our creative capacity to learn, perform, and contribute to the welfare of others.

Good luck, and read on!

1
UNDERSTANDING STRESS

a. WHAT IS STRESS?

One Friday the 13th, John and Mary got up late after a restless night, missed breakfast, and left the house only to find their car had a flat tire. This meant John missed an important appointment and received a sharp rebuke from his boss. On top of that, his assistant went home sick at noon leaving John with a double workload for the afternoon.

Mary fared no better. She was late getting the children to school. She had to cancel a hair appointment, and felt scruffy and out-of-sorts while showing potential buyers two homes she badly needed to sell. Another deal she had counted on fell through after she had made all the final arrangements. Still, Mary rushed through the grocery store to buy something special for their anniversary dinner that night. She was late picking up the kids, had a furious row with her 12-year-old daughter, and then got stuck in traffic. John came home exhausted and two hours late, and by the time he and Mary sat down at the table, they both had such grating headaches that they only picked at the expensive food Mary had prepared. That night, both Mary and John needed sleeping pills.

* * *

This scenario is probably familiar to most of us. For some, such bad days may be frequent. Lives filled with haste, worry, frustration, short tempers, anxiety, fear, tension, pain, and pills are commonplace, and the events of John and Mary's day are samples of experiences that naturally come to mind in any discussion of the word "stress."

Exactly what is stress? The late Dr. Hans Selye of Montreal, a leading expert on stress, defined it as the "rate of wear and tear within the body." A certain amount of stress, then, is perfectly *normal.* Becoming tense over difficult decisions, worrying about problems in relationships, suffering anxiety in uncertain situations, or feeling fear when in danger are all normal stress reactions. What causes medical concern and, thus, what we deal with in this book is chronic, *excessive* stress and the inability to cope with it. Dr. Selye used the analogy of body temperature. Heat production by our bodies is normal, indeed, essential. But body temperature becomes a matter of medical concern when it becomes excessive, rising above normal.

Too much stress, from either under or over stimulation, can lead to *distress.* Our minds and our bodies are in disharmony. They do not respond as they should. On the other hand, *eustress,* a term used by Dr. Selye, is a state of physical and mental well-being in which mind and body together achieve their full potential. A state of eustress (notice the similarity to the word "euphoria") is associated with clear thinking and peak physical performance.

Naturally, we meet and cope with many stressful situations without suffering dire consequences. Breaking a leg, having a minor car accident, finding the house burglarized — these situations are upsetting when they occur but can be dealt with effectively over time. The kind of stress that causes problems is usually more subtle. We are often unable to control or find relief from long series of irritating or frustrating events, for example, enduring a marriage breakdown, struggling to keep a business solvent through a recession, working under an obstinate and incompetent superior, or even coaching a losing peewee league hockey team. Over a period of years, constant tensions such as these accelerate the body's rate of wear and tear and can result in physical, psychological, and behavioral disorders. What is worse, while an accident and the anxiety it causes are easily observed, the growth of chronic stress is far less apparent. We are often completely unaware of the connection between chronic stress and our general health and well-being.

We shall define stress, then, as follows:

> A chronically high level of mental arousal and bodily tension that exceeds a person's capacity to cope, resulting in distress, disease, or an increased capacity to cope (eustress).

use this definition.

b. IS STRESS AFFECTING YOU?

Each of us reacts to stress in different ways. The degree to which particular systems in our bodies are affected also varies. To determine whether you are being bothered by stress-related disorders, rate your status for each symptom on the checklist on the next page with reference to the last month.

Research has shown that high levels of stress are associated with greater numbers of health problems. The average person will probably have a score between 40 and 75 points in a one-month period, and perhaps as many as 100 points for a one-year period. If your score is closer to 75 than to 40, you should review your experience to see if your health problems reflect any recent life changes.

c. HOW WE RESPOND TO STRESS

1. Physical responses

We mentioned earlier that stress is a normal part of life. In fact, humans are equipped with a specific biological mechanism for dealing with stress. This mechanism was first described at the turn of the century by Dr. Walter Cannon, who called it the *fight-or-flight response*, which describes the decision faced by a person who is endangered or threatened. This mechanism is located in an area of the brain called the hypothalamus, and it has been one of the crucial factors in human evolution.

Dr. Selye identified three stages of the stress response: alarm, resistance, and exhaustion. The alarm stage is when a *stressor*, that is, a factor that causes stress, is perceived by the brain. The brain sends a message to the pituitary gland which begins to secrete a hormone that causes certain other glands to produce adrenalin. The production of adrenalin sets off a general call to arms throughout the body.

There are many examples of the body's response to this alarm. In humans, the most apparent indications that the fight-or-flight response has been activated are—

(a) rapid pulse

(b) increased perspiration

(c) pounding heart

(d) tightened stomach

(e) tense arm, leg muscles

(f) shortness of breath

(g) gritted teeth

(h) clenched jaw

(i) inability to sit still

(j) racing thoughts

(k) compelling emotions

2

STRESS SELF-ASSESSMENT CHECKLIST

Use the following scale for each symptom and circle the number that best applies to you.

1 — Never   3 — Frequently
2 — Occasionally   4 — Constantly

In the last month I have experienced the following:

1.	Tension headaches	1	(2)	3	4
2.	Difficulty in falling or staying asleep	(1)	2	3	4
3.	Fatigue	1	(2)	3	4
4.	Overeating	1	2	(3)	4
5.	Constipation	(1)	2	3	4
6.	Lower back pain	1	(2)	3	4
7.	Allergy problems	(1)	2	3	4
8.	Feelings of nervousness	1	2	(3)	4
9.	Nightmares	1	(2)	3	4
10.	High blood pressure	(1)	2	3	4
11.	Hives	(1)	2	3	4
12.	Alcohol/nonprescription drug consumption	(1)	2	(3)	4
13.	Minor infections	(1)	2	3	4
14.	Stomach indigestion	1	(2)	3	4
15.	Hyperventilation or rapid breathing	(1)	2	3	4
16.	Worrisome thoughts	(1)	2	3	4
17.	Skin rashes	(1)	2	3	4
18.	Menstrual distress	(1)	2	3	4
19.	Nausea or vomiting	(1)	2	3	4
20.	Irritability with others	1	2	(3)	4
21.	Migraine headaches	1	(2)	3	4
22.	Early morning awakening	1	2	3	(4)
23.	Loss of appetite	(1)	2	3	4
24.	Diarrhea	1	(2)	3	4
25.	Aching neck and shoulder muscles	(1)	2	3	4
26.	Asthma attack	(1)	2	3	4
27.	Colitis attack	1	(2)	3	4
28.	Periods of depression	1	(2)	3	4
29.	Arthritis	1	(2)	3	4
30.	Common flu or cold	(1)	2	3	4
31.	Minor accidents	(1)	2	3	4
32.	Prescription drug use	(1)	2	3	4
33.	Peptic ulcer	1	2	(3)	4
34.	Cold hands or feet	1	2	(3)	4
35.	Heart palpitations	(1)	2	3	4
36.	Sexual problems	(1)	2	3	4
37.	Angry feelings	1	2	(3)	4
38.	Difficulty communicating with others	1	2	3	(4)
39.	Inability to concentrate	1	(2)	3	4
40.	Difficulty making decisions	1	2	(3)	4
41.	Feelings of low self-worth	1	(2)	3	4
42.	Feelings of depression	1	(2)	3	4

Total Score _____

Anyone who undergoes these changes is primed to deal with danger, challenge, or other real or imaginary demands. However, this state is temporary and reserved for response to extremes. The body cannot maintain it as a lasting condition.

Once the immediate threat is overcome, or after a person adapts to the disturbance, a reverse mechanism is activated and the body returns to its normal state. This is known as the resistance stage.

The exhaustion stage occurs if a stressor persists or if resistance continues after a stressor is removed. Damage, or even death, may result.

2. Psychological responses

The physical reactions just described are common to all mammals. But in humans there is, of course, the complicating dimension of the mind. Its ability to interpret situations provides an infinite variety of reactions to stress. A few of the more common psychological experiences, which vary from person to person and from time to time, are —

(a) inability to concentrate

(b) difficulty making simple decisions

(c) loss of self-confidence

(d) irritability or frequent anger

(e) insatiable cravings

(f) worry or anxiety

(g) irrational fear or outright panic

Stress is frequently accompanied by emotions such as elation, depression, rage, and fear, with the intensity of these emotions varying according to the circumstances. Expressing them can be appropriate, and can serve to cope with stress. Often, however, emotional reactions such as laughter, tears, or violence are consciously or unconsciously suppressed for social reasons. We may choose to avoid the consequences of expressing fear of a supervisor, or anger at someone we love, or even love toward another person. Unexpressed emotions, whether positive or negative, frequently cause stress.

Many psychological stress reactions become conditioned or fixed. For instance, a young boy may have a series of unpleasant experiences with people in authority. His reaction of fear becomes habitual. Years later, the grown man finds himself near

The fight-or-flight response

panic in situations he knows are not really threatening, such as being given a ticket by a police officer. His reaction is not to the present, minor stressor, but to the fixed one inside him. In a similar way, if we meet someone who acts unpleasantly, we may avoid that person in the future, in spite of visible improvements in behavior.

3. Behavioral responses

Stress may reveal itself in visible changes in behavior. Changes may include —

(a) smoking

(b) increased use of medication

(c) nervous tics or mannerisms

(d) absent-mindedness

(e) accident-proneness

(f) hair pulling, nail biting, foot tapping, and other mannerisms

(g) increased or decreased eating

(h) increased or decreased sleeping

(i) increased use of alcohol or other recreational drugs

(j) reckless driving

(k) uncalled-for aggressiveness

d. WHAT CAUSES STRESS?

Any situation perceived as testing us, threatening us, or calling for rapid change is stressful. However, not all stressors are negative. New love relationships, or important promotions can cause stress in a more positive way. Nor do stressors have the same impact on all of us. A job interview or an exam can be a breeze for some, but nerve-wracking misery for others. In order to be a stressor, a situation must be perceived and reacted to as stressful.

There are, nonetheless, a number of major events in life that are stressful to nearly everyone. Dr. Thomas Holmes and Dr. Richard Rahe have studied these life events for nearly 20 years. In one study, they asked 5,000 people from diverse backgrounds and occupations to rank specific life changes according to the degree of impact these had on well-being. These researchers found a high level of agreement among the sample groups as to which experiences they felt were very stressful and which resulted in minimal stress.*

After assigning a numerical rating called Life Change Units (LCU) to each life event, Holmes and Rahe worked out a life change score for each participant. Scores were then compared with medical histories. A clear picture emerged; the higher the score, the higher the incidence of disease. The more stress, the more illness in the next 24-month period.

Table #1 shows the Holmes-Rahe list of life events and the number of Life Change Units assigned to each one. Work out your own score keeping in mind that a high score does not necessarily mean that you are going to become ill; your ability to handle stress is at least as important as the particular events that occur in your life.

Holmes and Rahe found that people with total LCU scores of 150 to 199 had a slight probability of incurring some form of illness within the following year. Those with total LCUs between 200 and 299 were moderate risks, while those with scores above 300 were very likely to suffer serious physical or emotional illness depending on their capacities to manage stress and how much control they had over its sources.

e. MANAGING STRESS

Stress can be controlled. Excessive stress *can* be reduced and you *can* manage your stress reaction. You can learn specific skills that will help you identify potential stressors and modify harmful stress reactions without the use of pills, cigarettes, alcohol, or other drugs. Once you learn these skills, you will be able to manage stress when it

---

*Initial studies involved only males; subsequent studies included females too.

TABLE #1
HOLMES-RAHE STRESS EVALUATION

Add together the point values of the events that have occurred in your life in the past year.

Event	LCU
Death of a spouse	100
Marital separation	65
Death of a close family member	63
Personal injury or illness	63
Marriage	50
Loss of job	47
Marital reconciliation	45
Retirement	45
Change in health of a family member	44
Pregnancy	40
Sex difficulties	39
Gain of a new family member	39
Change in financial status	38
Death of a close friend	37
Change to a different kind of work	36
Increase or decrease in arguments with spouse	35
Taking out a big mortgage on a home	31
Foreclosure of mortgage or loan	30
Change in work responsibilities	30
Son or daughter leaving home	29
Trouble with in-laws	29
Outstanding personal achievement	28
Spouse beginning or stopping work	29
Revision of personal habits	24
Trouble with business superior	23
Change in work hours or conditions	20
Change in residence	20
Change in schools	20
Change in recreation	19
Change in social activities	18
Taking out a small mortgage on your home	17
Change in sleeping habits	16
Change in number of family get-togethers	15
Change in eating habits	15
Vacation	13
Minor violations of law	11

occurs and also *prevent* excessive stress from developing in the first place.

Stress management begins with a positive attitude. You will not be asked to adapt, adjust, fit in, or change yourself to suit others. Rather, in this stress management approach you are the central character in the drama; you will be the focus of change. Also, there will be no attempt to make light of any stressors affecting you. If something bothers you, it needs attention, no matter how trivial it may appear to someone else. Therefore, it is very important that you not underrate yourself. Don't feel inadequate because you seem to react more to stress than others around you. It may simply be that they respond in less apparent ways. Create and nurture a positive approach. With it, stress can be managed. Your health and well-being are worth the effort.

1. Basic requirements

The most vital requirements for stress management are *awareness*, *acceptance*, *responsibility*, and *coping skills*.

First, you must be aware of levels of stress, indications that stress is present, attributes in your character that may be stress-related, causes of stress and ways of managing it. After all, it is partially because of lack of awareness that stress-related disorders have become so common. It is important that you make the effort to be aware of what is happening around you, to you, and within you.

The second step to positive change is self-acceptance. What you are today is the result of all your life's experience. Change is always possible, but remember that important changes don't happen in an instant. Don't judge yourself harshly; accepting what you are and who you are is an essential step.

Finally, acknowledge that responsibility for change begins with you. Whatever your stressors — a noisy office, a bullying boss,

an unhappy marriage, an uncomfortable apartment — you can instigate the necessary changes. Don't blame fate, your father, or General Motors for your stress. Be responsible. Act. *Once you begin to manage your stress, chances are you can begin to join with others to change the sources.*

2. Strategies

There are four basic strategies you can use to manage stress:

(a) Build up general health through proper nutrition, rest, exercise, and other positive health practices.

(b) Change the situation; that is, the sources of stress.

(c) Change your mind; that is, your perceptions of, or thoughts about, stressors.

(d) Change your body; that is, learn to substitute relaxation responses for stress responses.

These strategies form the basis for the following six chapters. Each chapter describes a different program you can use to help manage stress in your life. The six programs are Personal Planning Skills, Progressive Relaxation Training, Quieting, Autogenic Methods, Communication Skills, and General Health and Well-being. These programs can be used independently, or together as part of a thorough stress management program. Choose the programs you are most comfortable with.

3. Learning the skills

Effective learning of a new skill calls for three ingredients: *awareness*, *practice*, and *feedback*. In the case of stress management, *awareness* is increased through reading this book, and perhaps other works in the reading lists at the end of each chapter.

As well, you must *practice* the new skill, or try out the new behavior, over and over again. Practice also may require careful planning. It is essential to practice regularly, especially at the beginning, if new skills are to be learned, as acquiring any new skill can be difficult at first. Only practice can make it easier and help to make it a part of your daily life.

Finally, the most important ingredient for success is *feedback*. Feedback means knowing what you're working on and how you're doing at it. Learning a skill without feedback is like driving a car with your windshield covered with ice. No feedback and you crash!

4. Demons

All of us have devils and demons that prevent us from doing the things we say we want to do — you probably know what they are. On the lines below, list three ways you would probably use to prevent yourself from learning stress management skills. For example, you might forget to read this book, or neglect to find a time and place to practice, or talk yourself into believing that this approach will not work for you, knowing, perhaps, that it has not worked for someone else.

_____
_____
_____
_____
_____
_____

Now that you have listed the demons, be prepared to deal with them when they occur.

5. The proper setting

It is hard to learn anything in the wrong setting. We need a time and place appropriate to the activity. Many people say, almost automatically, "If I could make time, and had a place to relax, I would not need to learn these skills in the first place!"

This may be *your* first reaction, too. If you spend a little more time thinking about it, however, you will probably find you can make some arrangements — perhaps with the help of your family or a neighbor — to locate an appropriate setting. This point cannot be overemphasized. If you do not take this step carefully, you will find it impossible to learn stress management skills.

In the following space, write down exactly where, when, and for how long each day you will practice your new skills. For example, you might put: "In my bedroom, every night, at 10 o'clock." Or, maybe, "In the den, every morning, at 9 o'clock."

Place:_____
_____

Time: _____
_____

For how long:_____
_____

If you skip this step by saying that you're not really sure of the time or place, you will be helping your demons defeat you. If you fill in the schedule right now, and stick to it for the next week, you will be on the path to effective learning. You can always change your time and place later but, if you do, be sure to write it down.

6. Support from others

Finally, it is very helpful if others in your family, those with whom you live, support your efforts to learn these new skills. Even if their enthusiastic support is not offered at first, at least have them promise not to interfere. This means that they must not interrupt you when you are learning your new skills. If they wish to make fun of your efforts, help them recognize that they are showing their concern and support for you in a very strange way!

CHAPTER 1 READING LIST

Benson, H. and Klipper, M.Z. *The Relaxation Response.* New York: Avon Books, 1976.

Ferguson, Marilyn. *The Aquarian Conspiracy: Personal and Social Transformation in the 1980s.* Los Angeles: Jeremy P. Tarcher, Inc., 1981.

Friedman, M. and Rosenman, R.H. *Type A Behavior and Your Heart.* Greenwich, Connecticut: Fawcett, 1981.

Goldberg, P. *Executive Health.* New York: McGraw-Hill, 1979.

Greenberg, H.M. *Coping with Job Stress: A Guide for Employers and Employees.* Englewood Cliff, New Jersey: Prentice Hall, 1980.

Howard, J. *Rusting Out, Burning Out, Bowing Out: Stress and Survival on the Job.* Toronto, Ontario: MacMillan Co., 1979.

McCamy, J. and Presley, J. "How to Relax and Reduce Stress" *Human Life Styling: Keeping Whole in the Twentieth Century.* New York: Harper and Row, 1977.

McQuade, W. and Aikman, A. *Stress: What It is, What It Can Do to Your Health, How to Fight Back.* New York: Bantam Books, 1975.

Mason, L.J. *Guide to Stress Reduction.* Beverly Hills, California: Citrus House, 1980.

Medical Self Care Journal. Box 717, Inverness, California.

Pelletier, K. *Mind as Healer, Mind as Slayer.* New York: Dell, 1977.

Selye, H. *The Stress of Life.* New York: McGraw-Hall, 1978.

2

PERSONAL PLANNING SKILLS

Undue stress occurs when we try to live up to an ideal image of ourselves. When unrealistic expectations clash with reality it almost always leads to frustration. Unclear goals, which result in poor use of time, leave us exhausted from heavy, unproductive schedules. Often it seems as if someone else is in control, rather than ourselves.

People who are chronically disappointed, frustrated, and worried may seem like extreme cases, but even the most well-balanced and practical among us wastes time and energy with resulting anxiety. This chapter covers eight personal planning techniques for improving self-awareness and self-control. Each technique is aimed at taking the worry out of worrying.

The first technique teaches you to analyze your expectations and beliefs. Sometimes we expect too much from ourselves, sometimes too little. By using *self-talk*, you will learn to assess your potential accurately and tune into *irrational beliefs* that are causing stress.

The second part of the chapter is aimed at controlling the amount of worrying you do. Practical worry control techniques are provided to help you reduce useless worry to a minimum. *Clearing* is a method of reducing stress by dealing with problems as soon as they occur. *Thought-stopping* presents a way of stopping the internal voices that keep us anxious. *Creative worrying* teaches a method of defensive worrying that very quickly defines priorities. *Problem-solving* helps you use the energy you have available to you when it is no longer wasted in useless worry. Finally, *goal-setting* and *time management* provide positive methods of moving forward.

a. SELF-TALK

Expectations and beliefs are sometimes inwardly expressed as *self-talk*. They may take the form of commands, such as, "I must never express anger toward my children." Some self-talk is perfectly valid, expressing moral beliefs such as, "I must not lie," or practical tips like, "Drive defensively." Negative self-talk, however, may reveal a deep-rooted irrational belief. For instance, if you say to yourself, "I'm positive I'm going to mess up my job interview," this may indicate a self-belief that "I *always* mess things up."

Irrational self-talk is highly stressful. If you say to yourself, "I must be perfect at everything I do," you are probably going to suffer from stress. Your expectations are irrational; mistakes are inevitable. A more rational expression might be, "I must try my best."

1. Analyzing self-talk

Taking a closer look at your self-talk can be helpful in discovering any destructive beliefs you may have. You can work to change the form and content of self-talk to reinforce self-confidence.

Recall a situation in which you experienced a good deal of stress. It is best to choose a situation where you remember making comments to yourself about your behavior. Sample #1 gives an example analysis. Then use the blank analysis form to assess your own situation.

SAMPLE #1
STRESSFUL SITUATION ANALYSIS

1. What happened? (When, where, who, what, why?)	Car in front too slow; I was late for meeting.
2. What was your reaction?	Angry at driver.
3. What did you say to yourself?	Crazy idiot! What does he think he's doing?
4. How did you feel when it was over?	Upset; heart racing; couldn't concentrate on meeting.

Now, fill in the details of your situation.

STRESSFUL SITUATION ANALYSIS

1. What happened? (When, where, who, what, why?)	
2. What was your reaction?	
3. What did you say to yourself?	
4. How did you feel when it was over?	

Think about the situation carefully, and decide whether your comments to yourself are fair or unfair. By being aware of your comments you gain control over them and can change them to manage stress. On the work sheet on the opposite page, make a list of the five worst situations that commonly occur in your life. After each, write down what you usually say to yourself when these situations happen. Next, develop new self-statements to cover the situation.

2. Positive self-statements

If you have trouble thinking of positive statements to substitute for the negative ones you use in stressful situations, look at the lists below. These examples of self-statements will help you to develop better coping skills.

Preparing for a stressful situation

- What is it I have to do?

- I can develop a plan to deal with it.

- Just think about what I can do about it, that's better than getting anxious.

- No negative self-statements, just think rationally.

- Don't worry. Worry won't help anything.

- Maybe what I think is anxiety is eagerness to confront the situation.

Confronting and handling a stressful situation

- I can meet this challenge.

- One step at a time; I can handle the situation.

- Don't think about fear — just about what I have to do.

- Stay relevant.

- This anxiety is what they said I would feel. It's a reminder to use my coping exercises.

- This tenseness can be an ally, a cue to cope.

- Relax; I'm in control. Take a slow, deep breath. Ah, good.

Statements for self-confidence

- It worked; I was able to do it.

- Wait until I tell my buddy about this.

- It wasn't as bad as I expected.

- I made more out of the fear than it was worth.

- My damn ideas — that's the problem. When I control them, I control my fear.

- I'm really pleased with the progress I'm making.

- I did it!

b. TUNING IN TO IRRATIONAL BELIEFS

Psychologist Albert Ellis has worked out a list of basic irrational beliefs that are widely held in North America. Through research and clinical experience, it has been determined that the more a person relates to the following statements, the greater the danger to a person's mental health. Do you hold any of these beliefs?

(a) You must have sincere love and approval almost all the time from all the people you find significant.

(b) You must prove yourself a thoroughly competent, adequate achiever, or you must at least have real competence or talent at something important.

(c) You have to view life as awful, horrible, or catastrophic when things do not go the way you would like them to go.

(d) People who harm you, or commit misdeeds, rate as generally bad, wicked, or villainous individuals, and you should severely blame, damn, punish, and scourge them for their sins.

RETHINKING SELF-TALK

1. a) A bad situation I frequently experience is _____
   _____

   b) I usually say to myself then, or later _____
   _____

   c) In future I will say to myself _____
   _____

2. a) A bad situation I frequently experience is _____
   _____

   b) I usually say to myself then, or later _____
   _____

   c) In future I will say to myself _____
   _____

3. a) A bad situation I frequently experience is _____
   _____

   b) I usually say to myself then, or later _____
   _____

   c) In future I will say to myself _____
   _____

4. a) A bad situation I frequently experience is _____
   _____

   b) I usually say to myself then, or later _____
   _____

   c) In future I will say to myself _____
   _____

5. a) A bad situation I frequently experience is _____
   _____

   b) I usually say to myself then, or later _____
   _____

   c) In future I will say to myself _____
   _____

(e) If something seems dangerous or fearsome, you must become terribly pre-occupied and upset about it.

(f) People and things should turn out better than they do, and you have to view it as awful and horrible if you do not quickly find good solutions to life's hassles.

(g) Emotional misery comes from external pressures, and you have little ability to control your feelings or rid yourself of depression and hostility.

(h) You find it easier to avoid facing many of life's difficulties and responsibilities than to undertake more rewarding forms of self-discipline.

(i) Your past remains all-important, and because something once strongly influenced your life, it has to keep determining your feelings and behavior today.

(j) You can achieve happiness by inertia or inaction, or by passively and uncommittedly enjoying yourself.

No matter what your unrealistic expectations or irrational beliefs may be, they can be changed. Stress-producing reactions can be replaced with coping responses. Two different responses to the same situation are illustrated below.

As you work through the stress management techniques, try to change your stress thoughts to coping responses.

c. PREPARING FOR WORRY CONTROL METHODS

Worry control helps us to empty our mental garbage. We can produce levels of stress equal to those caused by critical events and situations simply by thinking about them. Worrying about an exam or a job interview can result in the same severe reactions of sweating, heart palpitations, and nervousness that accompany the actual situation. Even the most experienced actors have butterflies just before they go on stage. However, as one person put it, worry control techniques force the butterflies to fly in formation!

STRESS PATTERNS

ex: college for name current event

Event	Stress thought	Stress reaction
Boss angrily questions quality of recent work	"Here we go again, more proof that I'm a failure"	Depression, low self-esteem

RELAXATION AND COPING PATTERN

Event	Coping response	Relaxation and growth
Boss angrily questions quality of recent work	"I wonder what he means; perhaps I can learn something here."	Feelings of mastery and self-confidence

14

Thoughts that constantly turn over in our minds, yet don't result in a useful plan of action are called *obsessive*. We may worry about our job performance or our children without having a concrete plan for dealing with them. Or we may be preoccupied with body reactions. Some people become excessively concerned with their hearts when they experience a mild change in heartbeat. Some worry about doing poorly in school, or about appearing awkward in new social situations. Many people worry needlessly about disapproval from others, about being punished, or about personal inadequacy.

All these worries have one thing in common: none of them does anything to solve the problem. Moreover, worrying should not be allowed to become a problem itself. This section describes how to prepare for learning three different worry control techniques: clearing, thought-stopping, and creative worrying. These techniques are explained in detail in sections **d.**, **e.**, and **f.** of this chapter. These techniques are designed to reduce worry and make it possible to take concrete steps to solve problems.

First, however, you must properly prepare to learn these skills.

1. Getting ready

When learning worry control techniques you, will find it helpful to prepare the proper environment:

(a) Time

Arrange a specific time to learn and practice each technique. This time should be consistent from day to day, otherwise you cannot expect to master the technique.

(b) Place

Arrange for a quiet and comfortable place to practice. Some people find that the washroom or their car is a good place. The place should be free of distraction from telephones, television, loud clocks, and noisy children. Being too warm or too cold will also interfere, so try to regulate the temperature. There is no such thing as an ideal place, but unless you have a specific place to use, you may find it difficult to practice. The main requirement is that you use the same place all the time and that it is as quiet as possible. Once you master a technique, you will be able to use it in any situation and any environment.

(c) Equipment

Make sure this book and the appropriate writing tools are available. Keep them in a special place, such as next to your bed.

(d) Body position

You must be comfortable. Some techniques require you to be sitting at a table, but if you don't need to write, you may want to sit in a comfortable chair or lie down.

(e) Relaxed state

Many of the techniques used to reduce worrying are best done in a relaxed state. One of the most helpful way of reaching that state is single-breath relaxation.

2. Single-breath relaxation

Breathing involves different groups of muscles in the torso. Some are located in the chest wall, a few even extend from the shoulders up into the neck. A large muscle devoted primarily to breathing is the diaphragm, located between the chest cavity and the abdomen.

DIAPHRAGM

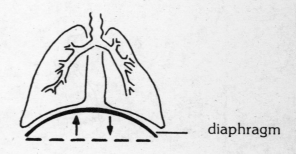

diaphragm

Relaxed breathing is done primarily by the diaphragm. The diaphragm moves a large volume of air and allows for slow rhythmical breathing. At rest, a rate of 6 to 10 breaths per minute is usually adequate.

Most of us, however, do not breathe primarily with the diaphragm, but with the chest. We wrongly try to keep our tummies tucked in and immobile. This chest breathing causes us to take in smaller amounts of air with each breath, so the resting breathing rate is closer to 10 to 16 breaths per minute.

Breathing in a slow easy manner with the diaphragm helps relaxation. The heartbeat slows in response to the relaxed diaphragm.

To practice relaxed breathing, start by breathing in as if you were filling your abdomen. Then let the chest become full as you continue to breathe in. When you are close to a maximum, relax and let the air flow out gently and evenly.

Your stomach will go out as your diaphragm comes down. Contrary to popular ideas on posture we should have an abdominal wall which protrudes gently as we breathe in.

If you have difficulty doing this breathing, practice by putting your hand on the abdomen. Your hand should move out as you breathe in. After you are good at getting the abdomen to move, then try to get both the abdomen and the chest moving. By starting with the abdomen, the chest will fill out naturally as you continue breathing in. You may also practice in front of a mirror after a shower or bath.

Some people habitually chest breathe and may require repeated practice sessions before being able to breathe properly with their diaphragms. Practice until you can do it evenly and spontaneously.

To do the single-breath relaxation technique, take a full breath as described above, and then as you breathe out say to yourself, "I am calm and quiet." Practice this repeatedly and in different situations until it becomes spontaneous. Don't be discouraged if you fail to obtain a relaxed feeling the first few times. Keep practicing — it will become increasingly more effective with time.

d. CLEARING

Clearing, the first of the three methods of decreasing the mental agitation caused by worrying, ensures that you either complete, both mentally and emotionally, each situation you encounter, or develop a plan to deal with incomplete situations. The goal is to clear your mind whenever concerns arise, rather than leaving them unfinished, and worrying you.

If you are clear of worry, you can focus your attention on the present, without being preoccupied with the past or the future. Clearing helps you become more aware of your present thoughts and behavior. Physical symptoms of worry decrease and you become more effective in dealing with your present activities. When you actually do need to consider past or future events, you will have the clarity of mind to do so in a constructive manner.

There are three stages of clearing. The first, carried out at home in the evening, is

PROPER BREATHING

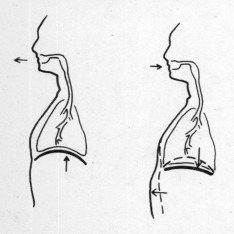

a summing-up process. It provides the practice required to do the second stage, which is ongoing clearing that takes place throughout the day, as required. Most people find that three to four weeks of regular practice substantially reduces their worry, increases their effectiveness, and gives them more free time. Stage three ensures maintenance and long-term success.

1. Stage one: Making a list

The first stage requires you to use the clearing work sheets provided in the appendix. Once again, consistent practice is essential to success. The clearing work sheets, if used regularly in conjunction with the following steps, will ensure your progress:

(a) Once a day, sit down, relax, and review your day, beginning with waking up. It is important to be relaxed. Relaxing allows you to practice thinking about difficult situations in a comfortable way. It also increases objectivity and creativity in developing plans for action.

(b) In the left-hand column of the clearing work sheet list any of the following occurrences during your day including —

    (i) Events that were particularly pleasant, interesting, or enjoyable

    (ii) Anything that was not completed, for example, leftover feelings, unvoiced words, or tasks not done

    (iii) Situations not dealt with satisfactorily

    (iv) Anything that keeps coming up in your mind

This exercise takes very little time. By listing the events, you are holding them at an objective distance. This process helps clarify thoughts and concerns and at the same time allows consideration of first impressions. These often are useful in developing plans. Remember to record both positive and negative events. You then will be able to deal with problem areas as well as reinforce positive events, and a balanced picture of your day will emerge. Sample #2 on the following page shows how you might fill in your clearing work sheets.

(c) Review your list and identify complete and incomplete events. Incomplete events can be recognized by nagging doubts, feelings of dissatisfaction, and prolonged worry about decisions and actions. Place a check mark under "C" if the situation is complete, under "I" if it is incomplete.

(d) Let the completed items go from your mind. They need be of no further concern.

(e) Do not spend more than ten minutes on this exercise; by the end of the first week you should be spending five minutes or less. As you practice, you will find you need less time.

(f) Select a time you can set aside to deal with problems that cannot be handled quickly and directly. For example, you may have a problem at home or at work and be unable to see a solution. You might plan to save 30 minutes tomorrow evening to develop a solution, rather than attempt to solve the problem while preparing your clearing work sheet.

(g) As you carry out each plan you have noted, draw an arrow pointing to the completed column (C).

(h) Do this once a day for one week, using a new work sheet each time. You will find blank sheets in the appendix, or make up your own modified version. Most people find that as they become better organized, they have an increasing amount of worry-free time.

2. Stage two: Ongoing practice

The conscious process of clearing throughout the day after each event can be developed after you have practiced with

SAMPLE #2
CLEARING WORK SHEET

PROBLEM, THOUGHT, POSITIVE EVENT	C (Complete)	I (Incomplete)	PLAN
1. Slept in and late for work.		✔	Set alarm.
2. Got a letter from Nancy and Mark.	✔		
3. Talked to Bob during coffee break about season tickets to theater.		✔	Call Arts Club for cost and info re tickets
4. Lunch with Jane — really nice seeing her again.	✔		
5. To bank to check balance in account. Overdrawn, worried about rent.		✔	Sit down after supper tomorrow & check budget for ways to reduce spending. No theater tickets!
6. Fell asleep on bus coming home.	✔		
7. Supper with family.	✔		
8. Talked to kids about report cards — concerned about Jim's.		✔	Call Jim's teacher re help with his math.
9. Read awhile.	✔		

your work sheets for a week. Before leaving any situation, determine whether or not it is finished in your mind, and, if it is not, complete it before you go on. As an example, spend a few seconds at the end of a conversation to review the encounter and prevent possible misunderstandings. Often a sentence or two is all that is needed. You can then leave, knowing that you and the other person understand the situation.

Now, use your daily clearing work sheets simply as a technique for checking your continuing clearing process.

The steps for ongoing clearing are as follows:

(a) Throughout the day, pause and check whether each event, encounter, or recurrent thought is complete or incomplete.

(b) If it is complete, you can leave it.

(c) If it is incomplete, complete it on the spot if possible, or, make a plan to complete it. You may find it helpful to make notes in a day book as a reminder.

(d) In the evening, relax and clear as you have been doing for the last week. If you have cleared during the day, there will be no check marks in the incomplete column.

After clearing, you are free of unfinished business in the form of worry, problems to be solved, messages to remember, and so on.

Once you become more relaxed and begin to worry less, you can be more constructive and innovative in solving problems. You may also find that you make better use of your time, and therefore have more time available to do the important things in your life. By the third week of the program you may not need to check yourself with an evening learning session. Then you simply maintain the ongoing clearing, integrating it into your daily routine and activities.

3. Stage three: Maintenance of clearing

In trying to change, it is easy to fall back on your old ways. To ensure success, we suggest you continue doing one clearing work sheet a week for the next six weeks. You also may want to review and read through this section from time to time. Complete the following checklist to help measure your progress.

e. THOUGHT-STOPPING

Our brains continually buzz with noise. Thoughts, worries, perceptions, even fragments of music, battle for our attention. Each of us is able to tolerate a different amount of this internal noise. While one person may require a high noise level to energize and inspire, another works better when things are relatively quiet. As a rule, however, most people have too much internal noise. Thought-stopping can help.

Thought-stopping will slow down the internal conversation you carry on with yourself. Breaking this chain of words gives you the opportunity to replace internal noise with productive responses. For example, in place of worries about handling an assignment poorly, you can substitute constructive thoughts, which will lead to greater self-confidence. And because worries can cause physical changes — tense muscles, headache, increased heart rate — we recommend that you think of relaxing images after thought-stopping to create physical, as well as mental, relaxation.

CLEARING CHECKLIST

	YES	NO
Are you clearing positive events?	☐	☐
Are you following up on your plans?	☐	☐
Are you doing clearing quickly?	☐	☐
Do you have a sense of completion?	☐	☐
Does clearing lead to better use of your time?	☐	☐
Are you better organized?	☐	☐
Are you able to clear on an ongoing basis?	☐	☐
Have you decreased your amount of worry?	☐	☐

1. Stage one: Learning

Follow the general instructions for getting ready as outlined in the worry control section. Make sure your clothes feel comfortable; loosen your belt or other restrictive clothing if it is distracting. Now you are ready to begin:

(a) Thought selection

Select one thought that you want to control. If you have trouble getting the thought to come to mind, force it. Don't be passive. This active effort is necessary if you are to control the thought or worry instead of allowing it to control you.

(b) Stop!

As soon as the thought begins to form in your mind, scream aloud STOP! As a variation, have someone else scream STOP 10 to 15 seconds after you indicate the thought is beginning to form.

(c) Visualize

Imagine the word STOP in the form of a large stop sign, or in flashing neon lights. Keep hearing STOP shouted in your mind.

(d) Calm

Now inhale, and when you exhale, say the word CALM to yourself. Let your muscles relax, if you can, and imagine a pleasant scene such as lying on a warm, sandy beach or watching a sunset.

(e) Repeat stop

It is often necessary to repeat the cycle of STOP and CALM several times in order to break the chain. Each time you repeat STOP, say it louder; shout it out if necessary. As you do this, eventually you will find that, while the original thought may return, it will begin to elicit the STOP image earlier in the chain. Although you may find some of the steps difficult at first, don't be discouraged; ease will come with practice. When you are feeling comfortable with the techniques in stage one, you are ready to proceed to stage two.

2. Stage two: Application

When you have mastered the procedures in stage one, you are ready to apply thought-stopping during your daily activities. The same basic techniques are used as in stage one, but now the steps are carried out during the day each time a negative thought appears:

(a) Say STOP inside yourself instead of aloud. You can yell STOP internally if you wish.

(b) If you have difficulty breaking the chain of words using STOP by itself, snap a rubber band against your wrist as you say or think it. This simple technique is extremely effective, and even though you may think snapping a rubber band is a bit silly, compare it to the absurdity of spending your precious energies on useless worries.

(c) Whenever a new worrisome chain of thoughts arises, take a deep breath —hold it—exhale, and say the word CALM to yourself. Imagine a personally pleasant and relaxing scene for 10 to 15 seconds.

(d) When you become aware of a worry or thought that is producing anxiety for you, immediately say aloud, STOP, and even clap your hands loudly.

(e) Now, think a pleasant thought.

(f) Get up and do something that will absorb your interest. If the thought returns, repeat the procedure.

(g) It is important to follow these steps every time and as soon as the negative thought appears. If you don't, the thought preoccupation will become stronger and more difficult to get rid of.

As in the formation of any new habit, you should try to practice thought-stopping at every available opportunity. This will help you to develop a new habit that will get rid of disturbing thoughts and provide stress-free relaxation. Perform this thought-stopping exercise until the STOP-CALM-RELAX-PLEASANT THOUGHT or ACTIVITY routine becomes automatic.

If you use the routine sometimes, and not other times, you will only make your old, negative habits stronger and more difficult to change. You cannot use thought-stopping half-heartedly. *Use it all the time or not at all.*

f. CREATIVE WORRYING

Continual worrying does not solve problems. If you must worry, do so creatively to find solutions to your problems. There are two kinds of worrying. One is useless worrying; it is unfounded and illogical, often dwelling on past events that cannot be changed. Some people call this creating mental garbage. The second kind of worrying involves constructive thinking and planning to solve problems. Often, useless worrying is confused with constructive planning.

Below is a series of steps that will help you develop your creative worrying skill over a period of three weeks. With effort, you can make your worrying much more effective.

1. Stage one: Learning

In preparation, select a special place and time to worry. For example, a kitchen table, a desk, or a park bench may be appropriate. The place must be free of noise and distractions. As well, make sure it is available at the same time each day. Commit yourself to a specific amount of time. Thirty minutes is desirable.

(a) Make a "worry list." Under "major worries," list the five things that worry you most. Then, under "minor worries," list other things you worry about less often or less intensively. Don't worry about filling the page or about exceeding the allotted space.

(b) Look first at your list of minor worries. If a minor worry can be quickly dismissed by taking some direct constructive action, it is not a worry, but a *concern*. Concerns can be taken care of by constructive problem-solving and should be removed from your list of worries. Transfer them to a list of concerns, if you like, but delete them from your list of worries.

If any minor worries remain on your list, you can still dismiss them from your mind. Remember, you have already decided these are *minor* worries and therefore you shouldn't waste your time on them.

(c) Now, look at the list of major worries. Spend the next 15 minutes, setting a timer if you have one, worrying uselessly about how each worry started, what it is like now, and how the future might look in relation to it.

(d) Stop after this 15-minute session. Do two minutes of physical relaxation or breathing exercises. If you find it difficult to shift from useless worrying to relaxation, use the thought-stopping skills discussed earlier to break the chain of worries, and then shift to relaxation.

(e) Now return to your list of major worries. With pen and paper handy, spend the remaining 13 minutes of your 30-minute session in constructive thinking and problem-solving. Look at each major worry in turn and decide whether there is one small thing that would lead toward its solution. Again, once you determine some action that will lead toward solving the problem, it is no longer a worry and can be removed from your worry list.

If you can't think of anything to do, put it on your worry list for tomorrow.

(f) Stop your exercise exactly on time, and arrange to go through it again tomorrow, same time and place.

The following are some examples of major and minor worries:

Major worries

1. Not enough money for a vacation.
2. Spouse drinking too heavily.
3. Too much work to do, not enough time.
4. Lack the skills needed to do my job.
5. Friend dying of cancer.

Minor worries

1. Dogs digging up the garden.
2. Kids fighting frequently.
3. Curtains need hemming.
4. Relative arriving.
5. Christmas approaching.

These are examples only; *one person's minor worry may well be another's major worry.* Remember: Your worries are major or minor according to how much they bother *you*. If something is worrying you a lot, it is a major worry, no matter how minor it might appear to someone else.

2. Stage two: Application

Review your progress in week one. If some constructive planning and some problem-solving has occurred, decrease your useless worry time by 5 to 10 minutes and increase your constructive planning time to 18 minutes. If you can see no progress, or if things have become worse, increase the time spent in useless worry to 20 minutes and decrease the constructive planning time to 8 minutes. Do not alter the 2 minutes for relaxation.

3. Stage three: Review

Review the results of week two. If progress has been made, reduce useless worry time

WORRY LIST

MAJOR WORRIES	MINOR WORRIES
1._____	1._____
_____	_____
2._____	2._____
_____	_____
3._____	3._____
_____	_____
4._____	4._____
_____	_____
5._____	5._____
_____	_____

further, with a corresponding increase in constructive planning time. Make adjustments as you see fit, but keep within the 30-minute maximum.

As you continue to practice creative worrying, you will find yourself not only freed from burdensome worries, but also able to organize and plan your activities with a new efficiency. Still, many people need a bit of help to solve their problems. The next section contains a basic problem-solving approach.

g. BASIC PROBLEM-SOLVING

Problems can be difficult to solve if we do not give them sufficient energy and attention. When energy is tied up in tight muscles and body tension, or in distracting thoughts or worries, we are unable to solve problems very well. You will find, having used some of the relaxation and stress management techniques described elsewhere in this book, that problems you found difficult to solve initially tend to take care of themselves. You can use the following five steps for specific, concentrated problem-solving.

1. Relax

There is a strong connection between problem-solving and relaxation. Every problem-solving session should begin with relaxation to help shift your mental gears and direct your full attention and energy to the problem as well as to open your creative channels.

The single-breath relaxation technique can be very effective for this purpose. Simply breathe in deeply and fill your abdomen with air. As you breathe out, silently say the words, "I am calm and quiet." Repeat this exercise three times.

2. Define the problem

The way we define a problem determines its solution. Although problem definition is the most important stage in problem-solving, people often limit their creativity by skipping this stage and relying on only a few standard solutions for most problems, such as getting angry, or blaming a particular person or racial group for their troubles. If the same kind of problem keeps recurring, chances are you have not defined the problem clearly; you may be working with symptoms rather than underlying causes.

When you want to define a problem, ask yourself some leading questions:

(a) What kind of problem is it? Is it a how-to problem? (e.g., How should I raise my children so they will turn out to be perfect? How can I get to Europe this summer?)

(b) What kind of result is intended? In other words, what is the least you will accept? Knowing this will help you evaluate possible solutions. If there are multiple answers, which one is the most important? For example, suppose you define the problem as "Not enough money to pay your bills." If the problem is vaguely defined as not enough money, then you are going to have trouble solving it. Maybe the problem is that you have too many bills for the money you have. A step-by-step comparison of the money and bills will help you define the problem more precisely. Exactly how much more money do you need? Exactly how many fewer bills can you arrange to have? Is the problem really money? Perhaps some of the things you need can be obtained in other ways.

3. Generate alternative solutions

Most problems have several solutions. Each solution may help us reach the bottom line, but each costs time and energy. Each solution will have side effects. For example, some people turn to alcohol to solve problems of anxiety and loneliness. This solution helps them reach a bottom line of relaxation, at least in the short run. However, excessive use of alcohol can be expensive, can lead to serious liver damage and malnutrition, and can interfere with work and social functioning. These costs must be weighed against benefits such as short-term positive feelings and less anxiety in social situations.

Alternative solutions to this problem might include joining clubs or social organizations, developing new hobbies, developing other stress management skills, or examining the underlying sources of anxiety and loneliness.

4. Evaluate the alternatives

Once the alternative solutions have been generated, evaluate them. Decide what criteria you will use to do so. Will you judge solutions in terms of their monetary costs, the time involved, the positive side effects, the negative side effects, their long-term effects, or their short-term effects?

Ultimately, we judge solutions in terms of their effectiveness and how they fit with our values. A nondrinker probably will not even list alcohol as a possible solution to anxiety and loneliness; a drinker will.

Look for one solution that stands out above all the rest because it scores high on all criteria. For example, the solution may cost very little and take very little time to implement. Clear-cut cases are rare, however, and if they are this clear-cut, a formal problem-solving approach is usually not necessary in the first place.

In most cases, we choose a solution that is far from perfect, but one we can live with for the moment. Our everyday language reflects this fact. We talk about "Making the best of a bad situation," or "It's better than nothing," or "Life isn't so bad, when you consider the alternatives." Quite often, though, a formal problem-solving approach can help us accept a solution we might not have accepted initially had we not looked at all the alternatives and found out that they were even worse.

5. Implement the solution

This is where most problem-solving efforts fail. We come up with a solution, but fail to plan how to make the solution work. In this step, we say to ourselves, "What tiny beginning can I make on this solution that will allow me to get started on it right away?" This forces us to build success into the solution.

If you don't plan how to implement a solution, or you don't follow the plan that you make, then you must return to the beginning of your exercise and re-define the problem. Perhaps you don't wish to solve the problem at this time. Ask yourself, "When would I like to solve the problem?" or "What will happen if I do solve this problem?" or "Suppose this problem didn't exist?" Such questions help sensitize you to the unconscious barriers that are raised when solving problems.

h. GOAL-SETTING

Excessive stress often results from recurring uncertainty about where we are going or how we plan to get there. No one has clear goals all the time, but everyone can learn how to clarify goals and begin to deal with the most pressing concerns.

Most of us are vague about our goals. We work very hard at what we do, but seldom take the time to ask, "Where am I going? How will I get there? How will I know when I've arrived?" Goal-setting helps us to accomplish not only the smaller tasks of daily living — shopping, arranging to take a course, getting the kids to school — but also the long-term goals for improving the quality of our lives, for enriching our experience, and for giving and receiving support and love.

1. Defining your goals

A goal is a statement about a desirable future. It starts out being general, but becomes more clearly defined as you answer the question, "How will I know I've achieved it?" For example, you may have the goal to manage stress more effectively in your life; later, you can make that goal more specific by planning to lower your blood pressure by 10%.

Goal-setting is a way of keeping track of your energy. A clear goal can provide you with feedback about your progress or lack of it. Goals change over time, but at least they provide a starting point. The more specific and tangible your goals become, the more likely you will be able to fit them into your available time schedule.

To be useful, a goal should provide a challenge but still be achievable. While difficult goals can lead to better performance than easy ones, they can, if too difficult, actually cause stress. You would probably be wise to try your goal out on a trusted friend who knows you well.

For example, assume you have a problem with elevated blood pressure. Your completed form might look like Sample #3. Now write your own goals using the blank form following.

SAMPLE #3
COMPLETED GOAL SHEET

My goal is to___manage stress more effectively_____

(write in goal)

by____December of this year_____

(write in a time by which you hope to achieve this goal)

In order to achieve this goal, I will_____learn how to meditate_____

_____

_____

(write in your action plan here)

Here are the observable ways in which I will be able to check my progress:

_____By having my blood pressure checked regularly every two months, with the
_____aim of reducing it from 160/100 to 120/80.

GOAL SHEET

My goal is to_____

(write in goal)

by_____

(write in a time by which you hope to achieve this goal)

In order to achieve this goal, I will_____

_____

_____

(write in your action plan here)

Here are the observable ways in which I will be able to check my progress:

_____

_____

Imagine yourself having already achieved your goal

2. Goal-setting and visualization

Visualization is a technique that will increase your awareness and creativity. It can also be used to increase the effectiveness of your goal-setting.

In order to visualize, you need to enter a state of deep relaxation. Try using the single-breath method described earlier in this chapter, or any other method that you find personally effective.

Imagine yourself having already achieved your goal. See yourself in the desired situation. Use all your senses to make the scene real for you — see, hear, smell, taste, and feel your goal. Don't worry about getting a perfectly clear image — it will come with a few days of practice.

In this relaxed state, say to yourself, "I have achieved my goal." For example, if your goal is to be wealthy, you might say, "I am now wealthy; I have all the money I need to live a happy and satisfying life." Or if your goal is to enjoy good relationships with other people, you might say, "I have a warm and satisfying relationship with John Smith. He and I care deeply about each other and respect each other."

Practice this technique two or three times daily for each goal. The best times to practice are just as you are awakening or falling asleep, or at midday just before meal time.

3. Planning life goals

People who have life goals live with a sense of direction that carries them through off days and temporary adversity. It is important to have life goals you consider worthy of your efforts.

Your life goals may be a way of life you strive to attain, an education and career, or long-range plans for early retirement and extensive travel. Your short-term goals will help you arrive at your life goals. In considering life goals, examine your present lifestyle, work, and home conditions. Are your long-range goals realistic? You may find it necessary to modify your goals to make them more compatible with your abilities and basic needs.

i. TIME MANAGEMENT

The person who lacks adequate personal planning skills never has enough time to do the things he or she wants to do. Life is disorganized and chaotic. Trivial matters burn up so much energy that he or she feels harried and frustrated most of the time. How often have you heard someone say, "I really would like to take up sailing, but I have too much else to do," or "I don't know where the time goes! It seems that I never have enough time at the end of the day to do the things I want to do!" How many times have you said these things yourself?

If you never seem to have enough time you need to learn how to be a *smarter* worker, not a *harder* worker. Being a smarter worker means being a better organized worker. The following steps will help you achieve better time management and, hence, better stress management.

1. Prepare a time budget

Use a log like the one in Sample #4 to keep track of how you spend your time for a period of one week. Brief pencil notations will do. This log will serve as the basis for your preparation of a personal time budget. For best results, you should carry the log around with you at all times until you develop your planned time budget.

Blank time logs are provided in the appendix for your use.

2. Review the time log

You may spend most of your time working or in work-related activities, or you may give a lot of time to child-rearing activities. Make no judgments about the positive or negative aspects of how you spend your time. It is simply a description. Review your log to help spot patterns that will give you an idea where you might find a little extra time.

3. Review goals and priorities

Determine how you would like to spend your time in relation to personal and professional goals and dreams. Initially, you should think about short-term goals, that is, those that can be achieved in weeks or months, rather than years.

You may wish to achieve a certain level of promotion in your job, for example. This long-range goal will be reflected in the short-term goals of learning specific skills necessary for the job, making proper contacts with those able to help you obtain the position, and producing the level and

SAMPLE #4
TIME MANAGEMENT DAILY LOG

TIME	ACTIVITY
MORNING	— breakfast — picked up dry cleaning on way to work — went to work
AFTERNOON	— work — took bus home — worried about argument I had with friend
EVENING	— made dinner — talked on phone — watched TV

quality of work required to qualify you for the job.

Arrange these goals in order of personal importance. Call the most important goals "A" goals, and the less important goals "B" goals. Within the "A" goals, try to specify degree of importance by classifying them as "A1," "A2," etc. You should have fewer "A" category goals than "B," and probably no more than five or six goals altogether.

4. Prepare an ideal time budget

Prepare a budget that will help you achieve the goals outlined in the previous step. Do not refer to your current time log. This step will show you how an ideal budget would look if you were to spend your time on the things that mattered most to you.

5. Compare your ideal budget with your current use of time

Now examine the gaps, discrepancies, and overlaps between the two budgets. This analysis will help you pinpoint the differences between your current use of time and your intended use of time. Examine the reasons for these differences. They are likely to include poor time management, lack of the skills needed to pursue your goals, and other time robbers discussed later in this book. This analysis should serve as a basis for the next step.

6. Develop a personal time management program

Using the hints and guidelines on the following pages, develop a personal time management program. This will help you bring your current time budget into line with your ideal budget. You may wish to revise your ideal time budget before embarking on this program.

7. Implement the program

Two weeks will give you an opportunity to test your program and to revise it if necessary. At the same time, keep a log of your time expenditure, paying attention to how your use of time alters as you go along.

After two weeks, if your time management has improved to your satisfaction, you probably can discontinue your systematic program and simply monitor your use of time every three months.

8. Prioritize

The key to effective time management is putting tasks in order of priority. Many people don't know how to set priorities; others are unaware of how to classify their various duties.

To manage your time efficiently, you need to be able to categorize your duties in order of priority. Make a list grouping them into *trivial, routine,* and *innovative;* or, *must do now, must do, desirable to do,* and *can wait.* You can then identify those duties that only you can perform and those that can be delegated. The next step is to set up a timetable. Use a chart, including time spent and to what extent you were able to complete each duty. You will probably find that failing to choose priorities is the main source of your time problem.

9. Eliminate time robbers

Your plans can go astray because of *time robbers,* incidents which, if repeated too frequently, eat into your time quite savagely. Time robbers include meetings, visitors, reports, and telephone calls. They are not necessarily wasted or undesirable, but they accumulate. Many people encounter these time robbers every day and fail to do anything about them.

Don't waste time feeling guilty about what you *don't* do. Set priorities among your tasks and stick to them. Ask yourself the basic question, "Will something terrible happen if I don't do this?" If the answer is no, don't do it. Schedule your time to include relaxation as a priority, and keep it protected.

j. CONCLUSION

In this chapter, we have introduced practical exercises that, if followed carefully, will help you to reduce your stress level. Each of these exercises is aimed not at stress itself, but at the causes of stress that we can control. In short, the techniques contained in this chapter should help you learn how to make your worrying work for you, not against you, through better personal planning.

CHAPTER 2 READING LIST

Bliss, E.D. *Getting Things Done: The ABCs of Time Management*. New York: Scribner, 1976.

de Bono, E. *Creativity Step by Step*. New York: Harper and Row, 1973.

Ellis, A. and Harper, R.A. *A New Guide to Rational Living*. North Hollywood: Wilshire Book Co., 1975.

Fanning, T. and Fanning, R. *Get it All Done and Still be Human*. Radnor, Pennsylvania: Chilton Book Co., 1979.

Gawain, S. *Creative Visualization*. New York: Bantam, 1982.

Lakein, A. *How to Get Control of Your Time and Your Life*. New York: Signet, 1974.

McRae, Bradley C. *Practical Time Management*. Vancouver: Self-Counsel Press, 1988.

Steinmetz, J., et al. *Managing Stress Before It Manages You*. Palo Alto, California: Bull, 1980.

Walker, C. *Learn to Relax: Thirteen Ways to Reduce Tension*. Englewood Cliffs, New Jersey: Prentice-Hall, 1975.

3

PROGRESSIVE RELAXATION TRAINING

Progressive Relaxation Training (PRT) is a self-administered program that will help you learn to be aware of chronic or habitual muscle tension in your body and to release such tension. Common causes of chronic muscle tension are emotional repression and generally high stress levels.

The fight-or-flight response discussed in chapter 1 explains our built-in capacity for preparing our bodies to deal with difficult or dangerous situations. Part of that mechanism involves tensing muscles. Thus, people who are frequently in high stress situations where their fight-or-flight responses are activated may develop a constant state of tension.

The opposite of the fight-or-flight response is the *relaxation response,* which is also instinctive. It is triggered by the *removal* of stress factors. In animals, this response is automatic: when they are not under stress, they are relaxed. Humans, however, can avoid triggering the relaxation response and remain in a constant state of tension. PRT is designed to teach you, or to help you rediscover, how to call forth your natural capacity to relax.

Medical researchers have found that chronic muscle tension is a contributing factor in a variety of health problems. Releasing tension can thus bring many benefits, including relief from arthritic pain, tension headaches, migraine, and other types of pain. Easing muscle tension has also improved such conditions as bruxism (teeth grinding), insomnia, anxiety, sexual dysfunction, and hypertension. Certainly, no method is a cure-all;

however, most people who practice PRT experience general improvement in their sense of well-being and increased enjoyment in many aspects of their lives.

Learning PRT, like any other important endeavor, requires some time and effort on your part. The amount of time spent each day will vary anywhere from a few minutes to half an hour. The training program can usually be completed in 6 to 12 weeks. As you master the technique, you will need less practice time; therefore, your commitment will be greatest during the first few weeks of the program. Learning to relax is a very pleasant task and your rewards will be well worth the time invested.

The PRT program consists of six stages:

(1) Preparation and beginning the exercises

(2) Learning the muscle groups

(3) Self-statements

(4) Combining muscle groups and formal integration

(5) Breathing and relaxing without tensing

(6) Review and maintenance

It is important to work through the six stages one by one, in the order suggested, and to complete the charts provided.

a. STAGE ONE: PREPARATION AND BEGINNING THE EXERCISES

In the first stage, you will learn to arrange good practice conditions and record your results. Also, the important activities of tightening, relaxing, breathing, and being aware, which you will use during all the exercises, are outlined.

1. Getting ready

Be prepared to practice two or three times a day. It is best if these sessions are in a variety of circumstances so you become aware of the tension that builds during your daily activities. Plan the sessions in advance and put them high on your list of priorities.

Times that have worked well for others include the morning before getting out of bed, just before breakfast, at coffee break, at lunch time, before supper, the late evening, and in bed before sleep. You will need to find comfortable places that are quiet and free from distractions. You need somewhere that allows you to close the door so that family, pets, friends, and co-workers will not interrupt.

Most people like to practice their relaxation exercises while sitting in a large, comfortable, overstuffed chair. Ideally, your chair should have a high back so that it supports your neck and head. If you do not have an adequate chair, you can practice while lying on your bed. Or, you can pile pillows at the head of your bed and sit with your feet straight out and with your back, neck, and head supported by the pillows. Try to distribute your weight evenly. Do not cross your arms or legs.

It is important to have a relaxed, almost passive, attitude toward the exercises. Do not approach them as if you were an athlete in training. Rather, imagine you are sitting down for a regular chat with an old friend. Don't worry about thoughts, sounds or other distractions. Even if you don't become relaxed, don't worry. You will progress as you continue to practice.

2. The tightening/relaxing sequence

Tightening helps to focus attention on tension in the body. As you tighten a muscle, you begin to notice how it feels. With practice, you will become more and more aware of any tension in your body.

Begin practicing this now by making a fist and tightening one of your arms. Notice the feeling of tension in all the muscles from finger tip to shoulder. The more you are aware of tension, the easier it will be for you to control it. Maintain the tension for

With practice, you will become more aware of tension in your body

five to seven seconds. You should feel no discomfort. Any area that has been injured or is prone to injury should be tightened gently.

Now let go of the tension. Do it quickly so that the muscles are immediately loose and relaxed. Focus on the feeling of relaxation. You may notice a comfortable heaviness or a warm glowing feeling. Take a moment to compare the feelings of tension and the feelings of relaxation to help you become more sensitive to both kinds of sensation.

Think about the way you breathe when you tense these muscles. Sometimes, when a person is tense, breathing becomes shallow and fast, usually because the chest and abdomen muscles become tight. If the tension is chronic, an abnormal breathing pattern can unconsciously become a pattern.

At this stage, breathe in a very passive way. Do not make any conscious efforts to regulate your breathing. As you relax, normal patterns will reassert themselves. This deep regular breathing is an important part of the relaxation response. Try to time the release of tension from the muscle group you are tightening to coincide with an exhalation or a breath out. You may find it helpful to imagine that you are breathing out the tension from the particular muscles you are focusing on.

Your awareness of your muscles and tension is very important when learning PRT. Pay careful attention to the feelings of tightness and relaxation. In the beginning you will do this actively. As you progress, you will achieve a more passive awareness.

3. Recording your progress

In order to keep track of your progress and to evaluate the benefits that PRT is bringing to you, a sample progress chart is included here (see Sample #5). The notes that follow explain each heading on the chart. You can use the blank charts in the appendix to record your own progress.

(a) Date

There are sometimes differences between our tension levels on weekdays and weekends. Noting the date can monitor these differences in your life.

(b) Time of day

Many people find it easier to practice PRT at specific times. Record the times of your sessions to reveal any variation.

(c) Tension levels

A simple scale has been devised to help you measure the amount of tension you are experiencing. On a scale of 1 to 10, with 1 signifying a very relaxed body (physical state) and a very calm mind (mental state), and 10 representing a tense body and a racing mind, note on the progress chart how you feel before and after PRT.

You may find that your body is at level 10, while your mind is at level 5. Don't worry if you find it hard to be precise; accuracy will come with practice.

The scale tells you two important things. First, it gives you a map of your tension level over the weeks. Second, it allows you to assess the degree of relaxation you are achieving in each session.

(d) Pulse rate

This column is optional. However, as pulse rate often slows as the relaxation response takes effect, you may want to record your pulse for your own interest.

(e) Hand temperature

This is another optional column. Hands and feet often become warmer during the relaxation response. To obtain your hand temperature, tape a thermometer to a finger.

If you use this procedure, be sure to keep the thermometer in place for at least three or four minutes before and after each reading to get an accurate reading.

SAMPLE #5
RELAXATION TRAINING PROGRESS CHART

DATE	TIME OF DAY	LENGTH OF TIME	PHYSICAL STATE BEFORE	PHYSICAL STATE AFTER	MENTAL STATE BEFORE	MENTAL STATE AFTER	PULSE BEFORE	PULSE AFTER	HAND TEMP. BEFORE	HAND TEMP. AFTER	COMMENTS
July 10	8:30 a.m.	20 min.	5	5	6	7	80	80	82	81	Trouble concentrating — children fighting
July 10	9:30 a.m.	20 min.	7	5	7	6	no watch		forgot		Comfortable — but still tense
July 12	10:00 a.m.	20 min.	6	3	7	4	78	72	86	91	Very relaxed
July 12	8:45 p.m.	15 min.	8	7	9	9	forgot		78	79	Interrupted — could not stop thinking about argument
July 13	9:00 p.m.	20 min.	9	5	9	3	78	72	81	85	Very tense to start — but became relaxed. Bad day at work.
July 15	10:00 p.m.	18 min.	5	2	6	2	78	72	no thermometer		Relaxing — memories from childhood came up

4. Three muscle groups

Now that you have learned the principles behind doing the muscle relaxation exercises, you are ready to learn the procedures for the first three muscle groups. Concentrate on the muscle group in the right arm, in the left arm, and in the chest, back, and shoulders.

Settling into your comfortable chair, or the alternate place you have selected, close your eyes and relax quietly for a few minutes. Be aware of your breathing and of your general state. Are you nervous? Generally tense? Excited? It doesn't matter what you are feeling. Just be aware, and then record your state on your chart.

You are now ready to begin the relaxation exercises:

(a) Let your eyelids relax and close.

(b) Tense your right arm. Make a fist, then tighten your upper arm as if you were going to lift a heavy bucket. Do not move your arm.

(c) Hold the tension for five to seven seconds.

(d) Release the tension as you breathe out. Let it relax for 20 to 30 seconds and notice the feeling.

   Now repeat the last three steps.

(e) Tighten your left arm. Be aware of each part of your arm.

(f) Hold the tension for five to seven seconds.

(g) Let the tension go.

   Now repeat the last three steps.

(h) Tense the chest, back and shoulders. Take a deep breath, hold it, and press your shoulder blades toward each other. At the same time, tighten your chest muscles. This is the only time you will alter your breathing.

(i) Maintain the tension for five to seven seconds.

(j) Let go.

Now repeat these last three steps.

Keep breathing regularly throughout the exercise, even if this feels difficult. Keep doing the exercise for 5 to 10 minutes. When you are finished, sit quietly for a time. Be aware of what you are feeling, and record your state on your chart (see the appendix). Practice twice a day.

When you stand up after your session you may find it fun and helpful to imagine you are wet, then shake yourself like a puppy coming out of the water. Swing your head loosely and quickly from side to side, shaking off the imaginary water drops. Do the same thing with your hands and arms, upper body, and your feet and legs. Imagine that the drops that you are shaking off are any last little bits of tension left in your body.

Do not go any further until you have practiced for two or three days.

5. Checkup

It is not uncommon to experience some problems after the first few days of practice. Any disturbances can be serious obstacles to your progress, so be careful to pick a spot that is quiet, and a time free from interruptions. This will make it easier for you to learn the exercises.

It is desirable, however, that you learn to relax in spite of distractions and interruptions. When you are practicing and you notice that your attention is on some disturbance, simply let it go and return to the exercise. This may seem difficult at first, but it becomes easier.

If you are having any fantasies, worries, unsolved problems—don't be concerned. Simply bring your attention back to the exercise. Occasionally you may have so many distracting thoughts that you wonder if you will get through the practice session. However, the mind usually slows and becomes more attentive to the exercise as you progress. If your thoughts distract you to the point that you have no more time, simply stop where you are.

Don't worry if you fall asleep during the exercise. Your body may require sleep. If this occurs too often, however, change the times or location of your practice sessions. You may want to supplement your regular sessions with one at bedtime, drifting off to sleep as you are doing it.

Some people find it difficult to differentiate between the tense and relaxed states of their muscles. If you have this difficulty, we suggest that you start off by tensing the groups very hard, then letting go of some of the tension; release a little more, and finally, let go completely. At each phase, try to differentiate among the different degrees of tension, and among the various tension levels and the relaxed state.

Sometimes, as one practices PRT, emotions surface that may have been held back for a long time. Do not be afraid. The appearance of these is normal and natural, and also beneficial to you. If you can identify the source of such emotions, it will be even more beneficial. So, if you feel anger, accept it, then return to the exercise. Or if you feel like crying, do so, and be glad of the release. You may wish to discuss your emotional reactions with someone.

b. STAGE TWO: LEARNING THE MUSCLE GROUPS

The ten muscle groups this program works with are—

   (a) right arm,
   (b) left arm,
   (c) forehead
   (d) eyes, cheeks, and nose,
   (e) jaw, lips, and tongue,
   (f) neck,
   (g) chest, back, and shoulders,
   (h) abdomen and buttocks,
   (i) right leg, and
   (j) left leg.

You are learning to tense and relax muscle groups to prepare you for your next relaxation session. As you continue to work, you will be applying these skills to learn the relaxation response.

As you read the instructions that follow for each muscle group, practice tensing and relaxing the muscle groups. Do so gently, breathing normally and holding the tension for just a few seconds. It is important to be aware of what is happening. Without straining, focus your attention on the particular muscles and note how each feels when tense and when relaxed.

After you have tried the exercises for the first time, take a few minutes to study your list of muscle groups. Try to become familiar with each of the areas and the methods used to tense them before going on to the next set of instructions. You may find it difficult to try all ten groups in a single session at first, but don't worry, there is no need to rush. It is quite reasonable to spend two or three sessions familiarizing yourself with the various muscle groups and tensing techniques.

Practice each group at least twice, with pauses in between. Breathe normally and time the release of tension with an out breath. If distracting thoughts or disturbances arise, don't get upset. Just let them go and focus on the exercise.

1. Right arm

Put your arm and hand in a relaxed, supported position and make a fist. Tighten your upper arm as if you were going to lift a heavy bucket, but *do not* move the arm. Now pay attention to the individual parts and consider the many points where tension can build. There are five individual fingers, as well as their various sections (finger tips, knuckles, etc.), the palm of your hand, the back of your hand, your wrist, the forearm muscles, and the front and back muscles of the upper arm.

2. Left arm

Follow the same instructions as for the right arm.

3. Forehead

Tension is often felt most strongly in the facial muscles. Every time you talk, smile, frown, or cry, you are using the muscles in your face. To tense the muscles in your forehead, try lifting your eyebrows high as if you wanted them to touch the top of your head. Another method is to frown, or knit your brows. Consider individual tension points, as you did for each arm.

4. Eyes, cheeks, and nose

Close your eyes tightly and wrinkle your nose. You may not wish to do this in public. Do not, however, be afraid to make funny faces.

5. Jaws, lips, and tongue

Clench your teeth, press your lips together, and push on the roof of your mouth with your tongue. Notice the tightening of the muscle that runs from the jaw to the temple on each side of your face.

6. Neck and throat

Pull your chin down as if trying to touch it to your chest. Now apply an opposing force to stop your chin. An alternative method, if your chair is tall enough, or if you are propped up against pillows, is to press your head back.

7. Chest, back, and shoulders

Take a deep breath, hold it, then press your shoulder blades toward each other while at the same time tightening the chest muscles.

8. Abdomen and buttocks

The stomach muscles are most easily tensed either by making your stomach hard, pulling your stomach in and holding it tight, or pushing your stomach out. To tighten your buttocks, clench them together, at the same time clenching the muscles surrounding the anus and genitals.

9. Right leg

Tighten the thigh, calf, and foot muscles. You may want to practice this exercise at first by tensing each of these separately. For the thigh, imagine that you are lifting your lower leg with your upper leg, but do not allow it to move. For the calf, press your heel down into the floor. For the foot, curl your toes, or point them hard at your head. Once you have done each one of these parts of your leg separately, it will be easy to put them together as one group.

10. Left leg

Follow the same instructions as for the right leg.

c. STAGE THREE: SELF-STATEMENTS

In this stage, you will learn to reinforce the tightening/relaxing sequence with self-statements.

1. Mind and body

As you are probably aware, your body responds to the way you think about it. A person who is confident and happy, for instance, will have a different body posture than someone who is chronically depressed and world-weary.

To help control these responses, we can give orders to our nervous system. Conscious control of the *autonomic* nervous system — those parts of your body that normally function automatically — is not as difficult to achieve as you might think. It has been carried to extraordinary lengths by eastern fakirs, who can order their bodies to sleep on beds of nails. (These feats are offered as illustration, not advice.)

Try giving your body orders in the form of positive self-statements about the condition of the parts you are exercising. The wording of the statement is very important. Try the words, "My (body part) is heavy and warm."

You may have noticed a comfortable heaviness creep into your muscles when doing PRT. When you relax, your muscles respond to gravity and you experience a sense of heaviness. At the same time, muscles in blood vessels relax and become more open. More blood is able to pass through and you experience a feeling of increased warmth.

By saying to yourself, "My right arm is heavy and warm," you increase your awareness of what is taking place in your body. Because of your mind's capacity for control, the self-statement works to increase the relaxation, reinforcing the tightening/relaxing exercise.

2. How to practice

You should find it easy to work the self-statements into your daily practice. Continue as you have been, but now, as you are relaxing and breathing out, silently, add the self-statement.

At the end of your practice session, finish by saying, "I am calm and quiet." Start using this phrase at the end of every session, and it will become associated with feelings of relaxation. As you progress, you will begin to be able to relax automatically whenever you think to yourself, "I am calm and quiet."

3. Concerns and questions

Of all the people who do these exercises, 90% feel a comfortable heaviness when saying, "My arm or leg is heavy and warm." The remaining 10% either feel different sensations, or do not feel anything at all. Don't be concerned if you are among the second group. Nature is still working and you are, in most cases, initiating your relaxation response even if you don't feel it. If you are one of these persons, carry on using the self-statements. They will enhance the experience of relaxation.

For most people, the feeling of heaviness usually lasts for a very short period. If you stay in a relaxed state, heaviness often changes to a feeling of lightness, or a feeling of floating.

Don't be discouraged if you are not successful in relaxing during every session. Things will get better. Or, if you find yourself short of time, practice for as long as you can; however, continue to note how relaxed you become during your sessions and fill out your charts.

4. Review

Before proceeding to stage four, take time to review your progress. It is important to master each technique before going any further. Fill out the checklist on the following page. If you can honestly answer yes to each question, you are ready to proceed. If you can't, review stages one to three and track down the problem areas.

d. STAGE FOUR: COMBINING MUSCLE GROUPS AND FORMAL INTEGRATION

In this stage, instead of tensing and relaxing ten groups of muscles, you will be doing the exercises with four larger groups.

The combinations are —

(a) right arm with left arm

(b) head and neck — including forehead, nose, cheeks, jaw, and tongue

(c) upper torso with lower torso — shoulders, back and chest, abdomen, and buttocks

(d) right leg with left leg

Practice the exercises as before, but employ the combinations of muscle groups. For example, tense and relax both arms or both legs *at the same time.*

As in previous stages it is very important to scan the individual muscles within each group. Be aware of what each muscle feels like tensed, then relaxed. It is also important to remember to breathe normally. Don't hold your breath. Continue to record your results and note any problems, new or recurring.

1. Quick relaxation in real life situations

Until now, all your exercises have been carried out in quiet, private places. It is now time to put your knowledge into practice in more demanding circumstances. You have been saying, "I am calm and quiet" after each practice session. Now start doing this at various times during the day.

Try repeating the statement in a variety of situations; for example, in your car at a stoplight, on the bus, shopping, preparing supper, or on the job. When you have chosen a time, just take a deep breath in, and as you let it out slowly and evenly say to yourself, "I am calm and quiet." As you repeat the statement, recall the relaxed feeling that you have been achieving after tensing. *Without* tensing, allow yourself to relax. Repeat the statement two or three times.

2. Formal integration

To ensure that you can do this in a variety of situations, list 10 situations in which you find it progressively more difficult to relax.

Start with one of the easiest situations you can imagine; for example, being at

REVIEW CHECKLIST

		Yes	No
1.	I am aware of what a muscle feels like when tense	☐	☐
2.	I can differentiate between tense and relaxed states	☐	☐
3.	I can relax each muscle group deeply	☐	☐
4.	I have noticed that I am tensing certain muscle groups during my daily life	☐	☐
5.	I have been able to relax all muscle groups equally	☐	☐
6.	I am letting go of tension as I breathe out	☐	☐
7.	I am able to breathe normally while tensing	☐	☐
8.	I am able to repeat the self-statements while relaxing and breathing out	☐	☐
9.	I feel a heaviness, or at least am aware of reinforced relaxation from the self-statements	☐	☐
10.	I have developed the habit of saying to myself "I am calm and quiet" after each session	☐	☐
11.	I have filled out my charts after each session	☐	☐
12.	I generally feel better as a result of the sessions	☐	☐

home alone or listening to some quiet music. Then, think of the worst situation you encounter. It should be something that occurs at least once or twice a month. Next, pick eight other situations that are in between these extremes, and order them according to degree of difficulty.

Over the next few weeks, practice relaxation in each of these situations starting with the easiest. Once you are comfortable with that one go up to the next level, progressing to the point where you can be relaxed in level 10 — the most demanding situation.

Sample #6 shows a progress chart for integrating relaxation. Use the format shown when filling in your own charts. Blank charts are provided for your use in the appendix.

e. STAGE FIVE: BREATHING AND RELAXING WITHOUT TENSING

By now you should have developed a considerable degree of sensitivity to the presence of tension in every area of your body. As well, self-statements should be telling your body what state to be in. It is now time to put these two ideas together, and to dispense entirely with the tensing part of the practice session.

During the new exercise, as with earlier ones, it is very important to breathe quietly and normally with deep regular breaths. Also be careful to scan closely every muscle in every group. Take your time, and enjoy the sensations of sinking into a state of complete relaxation.

The basic plan of the exercise remains the same, which is repeated here, with the new instructions added, for your convenience.

(a) Arrange for a quiet comfortable room.

(b) Record your pre-practice tension levels and note the time.

(c) Sit or lie down — take your time and get comfortable.

(d) Take a deep breath in, then let it go. Remember, you are *not tensing*, just relaxing.

(e) Focus on your right and left arms, one at a time. Become aware of any tension. Breathe out the tension and say, "My arms are heavy and warm."

(f) Do the same for your head and neck.

(g) Do the same for your torso.

(h) Focus on your right and left legs. Pay attention to each muscle as you scan first one then the other. Breathe out any tension you discover and say, "My legs are heavy and warm."

(i) Do all muscle groups in order, with a pause after each group.

(j) Assess your degree of physical and mental relaxation and record the results of at least one practice session per day.

(k) At the end of the session, say to yourself, "I am calm and quiet."

(l) Use the single-breath relaxation technique (see chapter 2) to enhance your exercises.

Continue to practice regularly every day, two or three times a day, and to record your progress. If you find difficulty in adapting to this stage, continue to practice combining muscle groups (stage four), perhaps alternating with self-statements (stage three) every second day. And, of course, feel free to go back to earlier stages whenever you feel extra practice is necessary.

Continue to record one quick relaxation a day along with your regular sessions.

SAMPLE #6
INTEGRATING RELAXATION PROGRESS CHART

SITUATION	QUICK RELAXATION ACHIEVED							
	WEEK 1	WEEK 2	WEEK 3	WEEK 4	WEEK 5	WEEK 6	WEEK 7	WEEK 8
1. Warm bath	✓							
2. Dinner and family	✓							
3. Driving in light traffic		✓						
4. At work — regular day			✓					
5. Dinner party			✓					
6. Meeting new people				✓				
7. Difficult customer								
8. Children fighting					✓			
9. Giving a talk in class						✓		
10. Writing an exam								✓

		Now	3 months later
1.	Improved sleeping		
	— fall asleep more easily	☐	☐
	— sleep more deeply	☐	☐
	— awaken more refreshed in the morning	☐	☐
2.	Less irritability	☐	☐
3.	More energy	☐	☐
4.	Clearer thinking	☐	☐
5.	Less worry	☐	☐
6.	Increased sense of humor	☐	☐
7.	More patience	☐	☐
8.	Increased efficiency at work	☐	☐
9.	Greater sense of accomplishment	☐	☐

If you have noticed other changes in your life besides those listed, use the space below to note them.

_____

_____

f. STAGE SIX: REVIEW AND MAINTENANCE

1. Improvements in well-being

After several weeks of PRT, many people begin to notice changes for the better in various aspects of their lives. Listed in the review chart on page 41 are a number of possible changes. To the right of the list check the appropriate column if you have observed this change. Three months from now return to this list and check the second column if you observe a change at that time.

2. Final checklist

We have now reached the end of our program on Progressive Relaxation Training. In this closing section, we would like you to review what you have learned to see if there are any areas in which you need help. If you answer no to any question, go back and review that section of the chapter.

CHAPTER REVIEW

		YES	NO
1.	I am aware of what a muscle feels like when tense	☐	☐
2.	I can differentiate between tense and relaxed states	☐	☐
3.	I am able to relax each muscle group deeply	☐	☐
4.	I have noticed whether I am holding certain muscle groups tight during my daily life	☐	☐
5.	I have been able to relax all muscle groups equally	☐	☐
6.	I am letting go of tension as I breathe out	☐	☐
7.	I am able to breathe normally while tensing	☐	☐
8.	I am able to repeat the self-statements while relaxing and breathing out	☐	☐
9.	I feel a heaviness, or at least I am aware of reinforced relaxation from the self-statements	☐	☐
10.	I have developed the habit of saying to myself, "I am calm and quiet" after each session	☐	☐
11.	I have filled out my charts after at least one session per day	☐	☐
12.	I am able to relax without tensing first simply by focusing and repeating a self-statement	☐	☐
13.	I am able to relax in difficult situations by using the quick relaxation method	☐	☐
14.	I am able to breathe in a relaxed way using my diaphragm when doing the quick relaxation	☐	☐
15.	I generally feel better as a result of the sessions	☐	☐
16.	I have enjoyed doing the exercises	☐	☐

3. Maintenance

Continued practice is needed to maintain and increase the effectiveness of PRT, and to ensure that you retain the benefits you have gained. To help you keep up your practice sessions, we suggest that you try out some of the following ideas.

(a) Support

Enlist the support of your family, friends, or co-workers. Tell them of your success and of the benefits you are receiving from PRT. Where appropriate, ask for periods of quiet alone. For instance, you might excuse yourself from a regular coffee break. Try to think of other ways of developing support for yourself.

(b) Reminders

It is easy to forget to practice, so put up reminders for yourself. Tape a note to the bathroom mirror, buy a special reminder toothbrush, put a sticker on the fridge, or write notes on the calendar. You might even subscribe to a monthly magazine; when it arrives, take time to assess your progress.

(c) Disruptions

Many times each year our routines are disrupted by vacations, family visits, Christmas, etc. If you plan for these occasions, you can work out solutions in advance that will enable you to continue PRT during such times.

Give yourself the generous congratulations you deserve as you succeed in doing each step of this program. It is a considerable achievement for adults to learn new mastery over themselves. Success builds on success, and being aware of your accomplishment can go a long way toward ensuring that the ability to relax becomes an integral part of your life.

CHAPTER 3 READING LIST

Mason, L.J. *Guide to Stress Reduction*. Beverly Hills, California: Citrus House, 1980.

Rosen, G.M. *The Relaxation Book*. Englewood Cliffs, New Jersey: Prentice-Hall, 1977.

4
QUIETING

In the quieting technique, ancient meditation methods have been refined and simplified. Modern medical research has shown quieting to be effective in controlling and reducing stress and associated tension and to be a preferred method for treating some medical conditions such as hypertension.

The basic requirements of quieting include —

(a) a quiet environment,

(b) an object or repetitive phrase on which to focus attention,

(c) a passive attitude, and

(d) a comfortable posture with the body supported.

The quieting method of relaxation consists of regular periods of rest, during which the mind is free of care and the body is clear of tension. This state is achieved by focusing on a special object. Some people choose as their object a flower, or a candle; others prefer a repetitive prayer, a word, or an imagined sound.

When the relaxation response is evoked, some or all of the following body changes take place; lowered blood pressure; slower pulse rate; decreased oxygen consumption; more relaxed blood vessels. The responses also can be elicited by other relaxation methods, such as progressive muscle relaxation, autogenic training, and certain yoga practices.

Quieting is based on a few easy-to-grasp concepts. As with all worthwhile endeavors, however, quieting requires dedication and practice if it is to be mastered successfully.

a. STAGE ONE: LEARNING THE METHOD

1. Getting ready

For quieting to be an effective method of relaxation for you, there are a number of conditions that you should carefully consider. These include time, place, disturbances, and posture.

(a) Time

Quieting is most beneficial if it is carried out twice a day and with a fair period of time between the sessions, for example, once in the morning and again in the evening.

It is not a good idea to use the method immediately after meals; an uncomfortable heaviness in your stomach or occasional nausea may result. As a general guide, allow half an hour after a snack, one hour after a meal, and two hours after a heavy meal. It is also not a good idea to practice too close to bedtime. You may fall asleep before the method can take effect.

An excellent time to do the exercise is between two major daily activities. For instance, after work and before spending the evening with your family is a good time. Relaxing after work refreshes you and improves the quality of time you spend with family and friends.

(b) Place

It is essential to have a quiet, peaceful, comfortable place, with no glaring lights and as much privacy as possible.

(c) Disturbances

The fewer disturbances you experience, the better the quieting technique will work. Therefore, you might want to take the phone off the hook, be sure that the TV and radio will not be turned on, and make an agreement with your family that they will not disturb you for half an hour. If the necessary privacy is difficult to find at home, you might consider staying after hours at work or going to the reading room of a library.

(d) Posture

Quieting is best practiced in a sitting position. It should not be done lying down. You will need a soft, comfortable chair that evenly supports your entire body — particularly your thighs, buttocks, and back. Your head may be supported by a chair or cushion, held in a balanced and neutral position, or be allowed to fall forward. Choose whichever is most comfortable.

2. The method

Having made all the necessary arrangements for privacy and comfort, settle into your chair, relax your body, slow your breathing with a series of deep, steady breaths, and close your eyes.

Now, think of an imaginary word or word-sound of one or two syllables, preferrably something that has no meaning or symbolism for you. Some word-sounds that have been found effective are: *shama*, *toma*, and *shreeng*. The Greek *hyrie eleison* is an historic meditative phrase that you may prefer, or the English word *one* also can be used. Its meaning gets lost in repetition.

Next, remaining in the same restful position with your eyes closed, repeat your word to yourself, slowly, over and over again. Do not say it out loud or form the word with your lips. Just repeat it in your mind; that is, think it rather than say it. Continue doing this for 15 to 20 minutes.

When you feel that 15 or 20 minutes have passed, open your eyes and glance at a clock or watch. If the time is not yet up, close your eyes again and continue the exercise until the time has passed. After two or three weeks you will develop a sense for the right amount of time and probably will not need a watch.

Do not set an alarm. The sudden noise can destroy your mood and reduce the effectiveness of this method.

While you are doing the exercise, you probably will find that your mind wanders away from your word to other thoughts, feelings, or minor disturbances. This is perfectly normal. When you notice that you have wandered in this manner, simply let go of the distraction and return your attention to your word or to your breathing. Do not try to push the thoughts or feelings away, and don't get impatient with yourself.

A slight variation of this method, which you may prefer to use, is to focus on your breathing instead of repeating a word-sound. If you choose this variation, select a point in your breathing cycle and keep your attention on that point. The easiest point to use is the slight pause that occurs between inhalation and exhalation — between the breath in and the breath out. Sitting restfully, just keep your attention on the repeated pauses between breaths as you breathe in and out.

You should decide on one focus or the other and to stay with it. Do not try to use both, or to alternate between a word-sound and a breathing focus. Much of the effectiveness of quieting depends on keeping the process extremely simple.

3. Passive attention

Now, begin working on the exercise in a *passive* way. We call this *passive attention*. An analogy may make this idea clearer. Suppose you went into a room for a while and then, after you left it, someone asked you if there was a light on in the room. You would be able to answer yes even though you had been looking for a book and had not actually noticed the light, lamps, or switches. You were merely passively aware of light.

Similarly, in quieting, you are not concentrating on your word or your breath, keeping it in rigid, fixed focus. You are merely passively aware of it, you are not analyzing, only aware.

4. Establishing a routine

Once you understand the quieting method and have tried it out a couple of times, settle into a regular routine for your twice-daily practice.

We suggest that you follow these steps:

(a) Record your starting levels on a progress chart such as the one illustrated in Sample #7. Blank progress charts are provided in the appendix. (See the previous chapter for detailed instructions for using progress charts.)

(b) Sit comfortably and close your eyes.

(c) Pause for 30 seconds.

(d) Begin to repeat your word or to focus on your breathing.

(e) Check the time (15 to 20 minutes).

(f) Stop the exercise.

(g) Pause for 30 seconds.

(h) Stretch.

(i) Get up slowly.

(j) Record your experiences.

Allow the relaxation response to occur, rather than trying to make it happen. We suggest you not try to make anything occur. Practice the exercise regularly and make notes on your experiences for the first few days. Also, record the time and length of time on the chart on the following page.

5. Midpoint review

We would like to remind you of two points that may be clearer now that you have had time to practice quieting. First, remember to think of your word, or to focus on your breathing, in a passive way. *Do not try to concentrate.* Second, when you notice that your mind has gone to a thought, feeling, noise, or other disturbance, simply return to your word or breathing. Continue to do this whenever distractions occur.

At this stage, you may be experiencing some problems with the technique. This is not at all unusual. Some common problems, and solutions to them, are listed here:

(a) Floating

Feeling that you are floating, or that your arms are not attached, is quite common and

Feeling that you are floating, or that your arms are not attached, is quite common.

SAMPLE #7
QUIETING PROGRESS CHART

DATE	TIME OF DAY	LENGTH OF TIME	PHYSICAL STATE		MENTAL STATE		PULSE		HAND TEMP.		COMMENTS
			BEFORE	AFTER	BEFORE	AFTER	BEFORE	AFTER	BEFORE	AFTER	
July 8	8:0 a.m.	15 min.	8	6	9	6	84	80	82	81	Felt like 5 minutes went by. Racing thoughts regarding work at start, gradually subsided — relaxed. Arms felt light and floating at end.
July 8	5:30 a.m.	18 min.	7	8	7	9	80	80	81	83	Became restless after 5 minutes, kept thinking of what I had to do. Tense at end of the exercise.

can be quite pleasant. Don't let it worry you. If you want to stop the floating feeling you can do so easily by curling up your toes.

(b) Bodily distractions

You may find yourself becoming more aware of itches or other minor body distractions. Treat these the same way as a distracting thought. Return your attention to the exercise. If an itch continues, scratch it.

(c) Too many disturbances

You may experience difficulty in finding the necessary quiet place to do the exercise. Try to overcome this problem by making any necessary arrangements. If the phone keeps ringing, take it off the hook. If your children will not leave you alone, get a babysitter or lock yourself in a quiet room. After a time, they and other people will learn to ignore you.

(d) Racing thoughts

Your mind may continue to chase after the concerns of your day. Don't worry if this happens; it often takes a while to learn the quieting technique. Don't become angry or frustrated with yourself. Keep returning your attention to your word or to your breathing. Quieting becomes easier with practice.

(e) Sadness

Upsetting thoughts or feelings often surface. Do not dwell on them. Simply let them go and return to the exercise.

(f) Nausea

Nausea or mouthwatering may occur as you get more proficient at the exercise. This is due to the onset of the relaxation response. Such reactions will subside as your level of tension decreases.

After you have practiced for seven to ten days, fill out Quieting Review #1.

QUIETING REVIEW #1

		YES	NO
1.	I understand the concept of passive attention and can use it while repeating a word or while focusing on the pauses between my breaths.	☐	☐
2.	When I notice that my mind has been distracted by a thought, feeling, or noise, I am able to return my attention to the exercise.	☐	☐
3.	I have a general sense of how it feels to be relaxed.	☐	☐
4.	I have enjoyed the relaxation experience.	☐	☐
5.	I have recorded my results.	☐	☐
6.	I have dealt with, or know how to deal with, problems of time, place, posture, and quietness.	☐	☐

If you say yes to each item, you are ready to proceed. If you cannot, continue to practice stage one for another week.

b. STAGE TWO: RELAXATION RECALL

1. Progressive awareness

At the end of your next quieting session, remain seated and focus your awareness on your body. Watch yourself, and see how it feels to be completely relaxed. Take time to go deeply into the feeling, noticing every aspect; your breathing, your pulse, your state of mind, how your body feels in general, and the level of well-being that you are experiencing.

The next step is to shift your awareness from your general state to a particular part of your body and notice the way it feels to be relaxed, independent of the rest of you.

First, concentrate on your feet. How do they feel? Be aware of them for a while, then slowly move your attention to your calves. How different do they feel now that they are relaxed? Now your knees, then your thighs, and so on up through your buttocks, back, chest, shoulders, arms, neck, scalp, and forehead. Don't worry if you do not notice anything special. Concentrate on being fully aware of how it feels to be relaxed, and get this feeling fixed firmly in your mind.

2. The recall

During the coming weeks we would like you to take a short break twice a day, in addition to your quieting sessions. Sit down, take a deep breath, then remember how it feels to be completely relaxed. As you sit, allow yourself to return to the state that you are remembering. Check out your body as you did before, starting with your feet and working up. Recall the feeling of being fully relaxed, and let yourself go gradually back into the relaxed state.

Try to practice this recall method at least twice a day — more often if you prefer —

and let the sessions last approximately two minutes. You will probably find that as you gain experience, you will be able to return to the relaxed state more easily and more quickly.

3. Keeping track of progress

For the next two weeks, make notes on your sessions, as you did before, for one quieting session and one recall session every day. Use one of the progress charts provided in the appendix.

c. STAGE THREE: SINGLE BREATH RELAXATION

Breathing is important in the quieting method of relaxation, just as it is in the methods discussed in earlier chapters. Review the techniques for single-breath relaxation in chapters 2 and 3 and integrate them into your quieting sessions. Use the charts in the appendix to monitor your relaxation progress.

d. STAGE FOUR: REVIEW

1. Improvement in well-being

After several weeks of quieting, many people begin to notice changes for the better in various aspects of their lives. Listed in Quieting Review #2 on the following page are a number of possible changes. To the right of the list, check the appropriate column if you have observed this change *now*. Three months from now, return to this list and check the second column if you observe a change at that time.

2. Continued practice

Continued practice is needed to maintain and increase the effectiveness of quieting and to ensure that you retain the benefits you have gained. To help you keep up your practice sessions, use the progress checklist that follows and the charts in the appendix.

To determine whether you have mastered the techniques discussed in this chapter, fill out the Chapter Review.

		Now	3 months later
1.	Improved sleeping		
	—fall asleep more easily	☐	☐
	—sleep more deeply	☐	☐
	—awaken more refreshed in the morning	☐	☐
2.	Less irritability	☐	☐
3.	More energy	☐	☐
4.	Clearer thinking	☐	☐
5.	Less worry	☐	☐
6.	Increased sense of humor	☐	☐
7.	More patience	☐	☐
8.	Increased efficiency at work	☐	☐
9.	Greater sense of accomplishment	☐	☐

If you have noticed other changes in your life besides those listed, use the space below to note them.

_____

_____

_____

_____

_____

_____

_____

_____

CHAPTER REVIEW

	Yes	No
I am able to focus on my breathing or repeat my word-sound.	☐	☐
When I notice that my mind has drifted to a feeling, thought, or noise, I can let it go and let my attention return to the exercise.	☐	☐
I have noticed that sometimes I have no thoughts, yet I am not repeating my word-sound and my mind is completely empty. (Some people regard this as the true meditative state. It may last seconds or minutes.)	☐	☐
I have mastered single-breath relaxation.	☐	☐
I have been able to integrate quieting into my life, and I can relax even in difficult situations. I am working on my list of ten situations (stage three).	☐	☐
I can relax deeply.	☐	☐
I am able to notice when I am holding tension and let it go.	☐	☐
I enjoy the relaxation exercise.	☐	☐
I have experienced some changes from relaxation response.	☐	☐
I have noticed improvements in medical symptoms or have been informed of a drop in my blood pressure.	☐	☐
I have been able to arrange for times and places to practice.	☐	☐
I have arranged for support from family and friends.	☐	☐
I have arranged periodic checks on my practice and progress.	☐	☐

CHAPTER 4 READING LIST

Benson H., and Klipper, M.Z. *The Relaxation Response*. New York: Avon Books, 1976.
LeShan, L. *How to Meditate: A Guide to Self-Discovery*. New York: Bantam, 1975.

5

AUTOGENIC TRAINING

a. INTRODUCTION

The fact that we can cause our bodies to relax by thinking in a certain way was noted by several physicians at the beginning of the twentieth century. Johannes H. Schultz, a German doctor, became particularly fascinated with the relationship between the mind and physical relaxation and devoted many years to developing a simple technique that could be used by virtually anyone. He coined the word *autogenic*, which means, literally, *self-generating*.

Dr. Schultz's technique consists of simple sentences that people repeat to themselves at particular times and places. The value of the technique has been carefully researched and fully demonstrated; autogenics has seen wide use in Europe, Canada, the United States, and Japan.

In the last 15 years, great impetus has been given to the use of autogenic techniques by the development of biofeedback instruments, which measure physiological changes that occur when the relaxation response is elicited.

The autogenic technique you will learn here uses sentences built upon three physiological states: a sensation of heaviness in the limbs; a feeling of warmth; and easy, natural breathing.

1. Heaviness

Special sets of nerves in the muscles of our arms and legs tell the brain the position of our limbs. These nerves are so sensitive they can detect the pull of gravity on our limbs when we are sitting, or lying down, relaxed. Most of us are unaware of this sensation unless we decide to concentrate on it, but the sensation is one of a slight heaviness.

In the course of research into autogenic training, it has been discovered that this feeling of heaviness can be induced by repeating a simple phrase such as, "My arms and legs are heavy." Such phrases are at the core of the autogenic method. When repeated several times they *cause* the person to become relaxed.

It has also been found, however, that about 10% of people do not experience the feeling of heaviness. They are, in fact, benefiting from the relaxation response without being aware of the usual sensation. Such people may still use the technique effectively because they *will* feel relaxed; however, they may have other sensations of their own, such as lightness.

2. Warmth

The reason for the cold hand syndrome in a stress situation is quite simple. When the fight-or-flight response is activated, blood is redirected to the large muscles of the body in order to prepare them for action. The supply of blood to other areas therefore is restricted. Small blood vessels in the periphery of the body (the skin) and in the extremities (the hands and feet) start to clamp down and coldness results. As the tension passes, the blood flow returns to its normal balance, and skin, hands, and feet start to warm up.

This warming up is the kind of physiological reaction that can be measured with the biofeedback machines referred to earlier. A simpler method, one that you may like to use in your sessions, is to attach a thermometer to one of your fingers to take a reading of your skin temperature before and after you elicit the relaxation response.

3. Autonomic and sympathetic nervous system

Autogenics helps you control your *autonomic* nervous system. For many centuries it was believed that the autonomic system was automatic and outside conscious control, as opposed to the *motor* or voluntary nervous system, which we can command at will. For example, if you think, "Kick leg," it kicks.

It is now known that we have more control over the autonomic system than was previously thought, although the system continues to function automatically if we ignore it. Thus, if you say, "My legs are warm," the phrase serves as a mild command to your body and small blood vessels will relax, causing an increased blood flow that warms the limbs.

4. Breathing

Breathing is another part of our physiology that functions automatically, but can be consciously controlled.

Breathing is also affected by stress. When the fight-or-flight response is activated, breathing is immediately quickened to supply the body with more oxygen in case sudden exertion is called for. Breathing also can become shallower as the chest muscles tense to prepare for action or as stomach and chest muscles tighten to control rising fear or panic. If the reaction is extreme, a person can breathe too fast — hyperventilate — which can change the chemistry of the blood and cause dizzy spells or fainting.

In a normal, relaxed state, breathing is deep, slow, and regular. In our third practice session you will learn how to use a simple sentence to help you restore your breathing to its normal functioning. This will reinforce the relaxation brought about by the use of the other autogenic phrases.

5. Benefits

Autogenic training can benefit anyone who wishes to use it. In the busy, difficult lives that most of us lead, it is extremely helpful to have such a technique on hand. The method also has been shown to be beneficial as a medical treatment for such conditions as insomnia, migraine and tension headaches, irritable bowel problems, ulcers, and anxiety states or phobias.

Please note: The autogenic technique is very effective, but it must be used with caution when certain medical conditions exist. If you aren't sure, discuss your concerns with a doctor. When you have done so, follow the instructions carefully. As you learn the technique, fill out all the checklists. Furthermore, the technique must be learned gradually. If it fails to work for you, it may be that you have been moving through the steps too quickly.

b. GETTING READY

1. Time and place

You need to prepare a place that is quiet, free from disturbances, and comfortable. You should aim to practice your autogenics three or four times a day in a variety of circumstances.

2. Phrases

Don't become too involved with the actual meaning of the autogenic phrases. It is the *process* that is important rather than the words themselves. For example, while repeating, "My arm is heavy," you may experience feelings of lightness. That is fine, and not an uncommon experience, so don't feel that something has gone wrong. For most people, this is merely an occasional reaction. As we have said, it is the process that is most important. The phrase is just a tool or a way in.

3. Posture

The two main conditions for correct posture are that your body is supported evenly and that both right and left sides are equally weighted. This can be achieved by sitting on a stool or chair with both feet placed the same distance in front of you, and both arms relaxed on your thighs. Let your head hang forward comfortably.

In this position, your body is able to completely relax. No pressure areas can develop in this position. For example, if you cross your legs, you could develop a sensitive pressure point.

Other positions you might try are lying down on the floor on your back with your arms at your sides, or sitting back in an armchair, with your head supported by the back of the chair. A variety of positions allows you to practice in a variety of places. You will probably find it helpful to practice different postures in different places before you begin doing the exercises.

4. Clothing

Loose comfortable clothing is important; a kaftan or kimono would be ideal. If you are wearing office clothes, take your shoes off and loosen your belt, necktie, shirt cuff, buttons, or anything that may cause constriction.

c. SESSION ONE: HEAVINESS

1. The phrases

The autogenic or self-directing phrases in session one are —

- My right arm is heavy
- My left arm is heavy
- Both arms are heavy
- My right leg is heavy
- My left leg is heavy
- Both legs are heavy
- My arms and legs are heavy

The phrases should be silently repeated. Say or think them slowly, and, as you do so, keep your attention gently focused on the part of your body to which the phrase refers. Repeat each phrase one or more times, with pauses in between. Always start with the phrase, "My right arm is heavy." If you are left-handed, however, you may prefer to begin with your left arm. If this is the case, be consistent; always start with your left arm.

When you begin to practice, use one phrase only. For instance, just say, "My right arm is heavy." Try this out and see how it suits you. If you find that a relaxed, comfortable, heavy feeling is being generated and is flowing to your other limbs, obviously the single phrase works well for you. After a few days, you may be ready to move on to another limb.

When you are saying all the phrases, a practice session may last three to five minutes. If only one is being used, the time will be shorter, as little as twenty to thirty seconds.

2. Awareness

The *passive awareness* attitude is very important to maintain. At the same time, passivity should not be taken to mean inattention to your bodily state. It is your awareness that is directing the flow of command to your limbs. So make sure that your awareness is held on the body part in question; you should be aware of it, of what it is feeling, and of what is taking place.

3. Breathing

In autogenic or self-directed relaxation, breathing during the practice session should be done passively. Do not control your breathing or change it in any way. Just allow it to occur while you are doing the exercise. In fact, if your mind goes to your breathing, treat it as you would any other distracting thought. Simply allow your attention to return to the self-directing phrase.

4. Recording

Practice autogenics without expectation of the results. Record what occurs to you during autogenics for the first three days. Put the date, time, and length of time you are practicing in Sample #8. If after the first three days, you begin to feel the heaviness flowing to other parts of your body, begin to add the additional phrases. Continue to monitor your progress using the blank progress charts provided in the appendix.

5. Establishing a routine

Once you understand the method and have tried it out a couple of times, it is helpful if you settle into a routine for your daily practice. Follow these steps:

(a) Find a quiet, comfortable place and either sit or lie down.

(b) Record your state on the chart provided in the appendix.

(c) Check your posture and spend a little time ensuring that it is correct.

(d) Close your eyes; pause for a few seconds.

(e) Take a deep breath in, a full breath — using both the abdomen and the chest — and then let it flow out, neither pushing it nor holding it back.

(f) Begin your self-directing phrases with "My right arm is heavy." Say each phrase one or more times, with pauses between the phrases.

(g) Continue with the remaining phrases: right arm; both arms; right leg; left leg; both legs; both arms and legs together.

(h) As you repeat the phrases, be passively aware of the sensations in your limbs.

(i) When you have finished repeating the phrases, make fists, tighten up both arms and flex them; take a deep breath in.

(j) Breathe out, and open your eyes as you relax both arms.

(k) Record your state on your chart.

6. Review

When you have practiced session one for a few days, fill out the following review as a measure of your progress and understanding.

AUTOGENICS REVIEW #1

		Yes	No
1.	I understand what is meant by an autogenic or self-directing phrase.	☐	☐
2.	I understand the relationship between the phrases and the changes that can occur in my body.	☐	☐
3.	I understand that the phrases are tools with which to achieve an overall relaxation response.	☐	☐
4.	I understand the need for a passive attitude when doing the exercise.	☐	☐
5.	I am able to return my attention to the exercise when distractions occur.	☐	☐
6.	I recognize the importance of a suitable time, place, and posture.	☐	☐
7.	I understand the need to record my state and progress.	☐	☐
8.	I have established a routine and do the exercise as a series of steps.	☐	☐

SAMPLE #8
AUTOGENICS PROGRESS CHART

DATE	TIME OF DAY	LENGTH OF TIME	PHYSICAL STATE BEFORE	PHYSICAL STATE AFTER	MENTAL STATE BEFORE	MENTAL STATE AFTER	PULSE BEFORE	PULSE AFTER	HAND TEMP. BEFORE	HAND TEMP. AFTER	COMMENTS
July 8	8:00 a.m.	1 min.	6	7	8	6	80	80		forgot	Feeling rushed, but relaxed after getting into correct posture. Arms felt comfortable — heaviness not experienced.
July 8	5:30 p.m.	3 min.	4	6	3	7	78	77	85	83	Repeated phrase 5 times, noticed slight heaviness. Foot jerked, some heaviness in other limbs, pressure in forehead.

56

d. SESSION TWO: WARMTH

In this session we cover two new autogenic phrases. The first expresses the experience of warmth during relaxation. The second expresses a general relaxation statement to be used in any tense situation and at the end of each practice session.

1. The phrases

The new autogenic phrases for this session are —

- My right arm is warm
- My left arm is warm
- Both arms are warm
- My right leg is warm
- My left leg is warm
- Both legs are warm
- My arms and legs are warm

Do the exercise in the same manner as session one, with the same pacing, passive awareness, and breathing rhythm. Continue saying the phrases from session one before you start these new phrases. If you repeat each phrase three times with pauses in between, the whole exercise will take seven to ten minutes. Try to practice at least three times a day.

2. Undue warmth

If you should find that your limbs are becoming too warm or too heavy, alter the phrase by inserting the word "comfortably." Thus, "My right arm is comfortably warm," "My left leg is comfortably heavy." This alteration should limit the response so that you are relaxed, yet comfortable.

3. Unaccustomed sensations

Many people experience new sensations while doing autogenic training. Such sensations are quite normal and indicate that your training is proving effective. Some of them might be —

- a feeling of detachment of the arms or legs,

- a feeling of numbness or decreased sensitivity of the arms,
- a feeling of weakness,
- a tingling or twitching of the arms, or
- a feeling of floating, or a feeling that the arm is two to three times its normal size.

Don't let these sensations bother you. Actually, they are normal and pleasant when you are familiar with them.

4. New general phrase

Now, introduce a new general autogenic statement at the end of each practice session. The phrase is, "My neck and shoulders are heavy."

The statement is built — in the same manner as the others — from the general observation that when you are relaxed a feeling of comfortable heaviness can be detected. The shoulders and neck are also among the most common places for tension to develop. The self-directing phrase, "My neck and shoulders are heavy" directs relaxation to a significant place.

End every practice session with this new phrase. It will come to be associated with the relaxation you have won by patient repetition of the first two sets of autogenic phrases.

After you have introduced this phrase into your sessions, try using it at various times in your daily life when you experience tension or whenever you feel like relaxing.

For example, if you are driving in heavy traffic and you come to a stop sign, you can repeat to yourself, "My neck and shoulders are heavy," and relax yourself. Or, if you are talking to somebody and feel yourself getting uptight, you can, even while he or she is talking to you, repeat to yourself, "My neck and shoulders are heavy" and relax. The phrase thus begins to act as a cue for you to relax in any trying situation.

Practice using this phrase randomly over the next week.

Complete Autogenics Review #2 as a measure of your progress and understanding when you have mastered session two.

e. SESSION THREE: BREATHING

This breathing session is more subtle and somewhat more complex than sessions one or two, although it has the same underlying pattern: thought — mild command — bodily change.

The first thing to remember is not to become unduly conscious of your breathing. Don't ask yourself, "Is my breathing fast, slow, deep, or shallow?" Don't actually think about your breathing at all. Just be passively aware of what is taking place in your body, and allow your breathing to take care of itself.

1. The phrases

The phrase to be used is, "My body breathes me." Repeat this phrase several times. Insert it into the exercise after you have repeated, "My arms and legs are warm," before you finish the exercise with, "My neck and shoulders are heavy."

For your reference, here is the complete list of phrases that you will be using this session.

- My right arm is heavy
- My left arm is heavy
- Both arms are heavy
- My right leg is heavy
- My left leg is heavy
- Both legs are heavy
- My arms and legs are heavy
- My right arm is warm
- My left arm is warm
- Both arms are warm
- My right leg is warm
- My left leg is warm
- Both legs are warm
- My arms and legs are warm
- My body breathes me
- My neck and shoulders are heavy

AUTOGENICS REVIEW #2

		Yes	No
1.	I understand the rationale behind the second formula, "My right arm is warm."	☐	☐
2.	I understand the addition, "My neck and shoulders are heavy."	☐	☐
3.	I understand the development of the cue phrase, "My neck and shoulders are heavy," to elicit the relaxation response while doing other activities.	☐	☐
4.	I will practice doing the cue phrase while doing other activities.	☐	☐
5.	I have arranged support time and a place to practice over the next 7 to 10 days.	☐	☐

Try using your autogenic phrase at various times in your daily life when you experience tension

2. The steps

Follow the same sequence of steps as in the previous sessions. Here they are again:

(a) Arrange time, place, posture.

(b) Record your state.

(c) Take a deep breath, close your eyes.

(d) Repeat heavy phrases one or more times.

(e) Repeat warm phrases one or more times.

(f) Repeat "My body breathes me," one or more times.

(g) Say "My neck and shoulders are heavy."

(h) Make fists, flex your arms, breathe in, relax, breathe out, open your eyes.

(i) Record the progress of at least one of your sessions a day.

3. Prolonging the exercise

Sometimes when you are practicing autogenics, you may find yourself perfectly content where you are and feel that you would like to carry on doing the exercise. Or, you may feel that you need a good rest in the course of the day, but have only 15 minutes to spare.

If you wish to prolong your sessions, or need a good but short rest, try this:

(a) Do the complete session exercise until you get to "My neck and shoulders are heavy."

(b) Instead of finishing, start to focus your attention gently and passively on the pauses that occur regularly between each breath.

(c) Continue to breathe in the passive, relaxed manner; that is, without concentrating on your breathing. Keep your attention on the repeated pauses between your inhalations and exhalations.

(d) Keep this up for 5 to 15 minutes.

(e) To time yourself, set a clock or watch at eye level. When you think 15 minutes have passed, open your eyes. If the time isn't up, just close your eyes and return your attention to the pauses between your breaths. Do not set an alarm or get up to look at a clock, as this can destroy the purpose of the exercise.

(f) Remember to end with "My neck and shoulders are heavy."

4. Practicing three ways

We have now covered three different approaches to the use of autogenic phrases. First, the regular session covered heaviness, warmth, and breathing. Then, the quick relaxation method used the cue phrase, "My neck and shoulders are heavy." The last method is the prolonged session in which you focused on the pauses in your breathing for 15 to 20 minutes.

In the course of the next two weeks, practice each type of exercise every day. A recommended schedule is —

- Quick exercise — 3 to 5 times or more
- Regular exercise — 1 to 2 times
- Prolonged exercise — once daily

Although this schedule asks for a fairly big commitment of time and effort, try to carry out the whole program. We think you will find the end results are worth it.

5. Checklist

When you have practiced the three-way program of autogenics for two or three days, fill out Autogenics Review #3 below as a measure of your progress and understanding.

f. SESSION FOUR: INTEGRATION

We asked you earlier to start using the cue phrase, "My neck and shoulders are heavy" at various times of day. Now, start using this more specifically in situations that make you tense, or in which you habitually suffer severe stress reactions. Use one of the integrating relaxation charts in the appendix to record your progress.

Make a list of 10 situations that occur regularly in your life in which you find it difficult to relax. Start with the easiest and end with the most difficult. If you can't think of 10 different situations, just list as many as you know. When you have made the list, start practicing with the cue phrase whenever any one of your first three situations occur. When you can relax in the first situation, you should begin practicing with the second, third, and fourth; then the third, fourth, and fifth. Continue until you have mastered every situation on your list.

Practice using the cue phrase for two weeks. This practice is sometimes a very difficult part of the technique to master because, naturally enough, most of our attention is on the factor that is causing us stress.

AUTOGENICS REVIEW #3

		Yes	No
1.	I understand breathing as it relates to stress.	☐	☐
2.	I understand how self-directing phrases can help normalize my breathing pattern.	☐	☐
3.	I understand and use the regular exercise including the phrase "My body breathes me."	☐	☐
4.	I understand how to prolong the exercise by passively focusing on the pauses between my breaths.	☐	☐
5.	I use the quick relaxation method several times a day.	☐	☐
6.	I am recording my results.	☐	☐

		Yes	No
1.	I can increase or decrease the time of doing my exercise to suit the time and place.	☐	☐
2.	I understand the special formulas.	☐	☐
3.	I understand the use of the formula, "My neck and shoulders are heavy," in the integration process.	☐	☐
4.	I understand the importance of practicing, "My neck and shoulders are heavy," in progressively more difficult situations.	☐	☐

When you have mastered session four, fill out Autogenics Review #4 at the top of this page as a measure of your progress and understanding.

g. SESSION FIVE: REVIEW

1. Improvement in well-being

After several weeks of autogenics, many people begin to notice changes for the better in various aspects of their lives. Complete the Chapter Review now, and then again in three months' time, as some changes occur very gradually.

2. Continued practice

Continued practice is needed to maintain and increase the effectiveness of autogenics and to ensure that you retain the benefits you have gained. Use the progress charts in the appendix to help you keep on track.

Record one autogenic session every other day for the next eight weeks. Every two or three weeks, compare your more recent progress records with your earlier ones. If you experience any problems, try going back over the chapter and all your notes.

CHAPTER REVIEW

		Now	3 months later
1.	Improved sleeping		
	—fall asleep more easily	☐	☐
	—sleep more deeply	☐	☐
	—awaken more refreshed in the morning	☐	☐
2.	Less irritability	☐	☐
3.	More energy	☐	☐
4.	Clearer thinking	☐	☐
5.	Less worry	☐	☐
6.	Increased sense of humor	☐	☐
7.	More patience	☐	☐
8.	Increased efficiency at work	☐	☐
9.	Greater sense of accomplishment	☐	☐

If you have noticed other changes in your life besides those listed, use the space below to note them.

_____

_____

_____

_____

_____

_____

_____

CHAPTER 5 READING LIST

Mason, L.J. *Guide to Stress Reduction*. Beverly Hills, California: Citrus House, 1980.

Pelletier, K. *Mind as Healer, Mind as Slayer*. New York: Dell, 1977.

6
COMMUNICATION SKILLS

Many stress management skills such as relaxation training, quieting, or autogenics, involve only ourselves. We can regain a feeling of control over stress reactions by learning these techniques without necessarily interacting with others. Communication skills address our interaction with others.

This chapter is for people whose sources of excessive stress include their interactions with others. The skills learned will be useful in managing undue stress while communicating generally, and within important relationships with employers, spouse, or children.

Once you develop the necessary skills, your communication is effective, leaving little room for misunderstanding and the stress it produces. Without communication skills, however, incomplete messages may be relayed, with a resulting increase in stress. For example, if the sender of a message has had a bad day and is feeling thoroughly frustrated, that person might say, "I can't stand it here any longer!" The receiver, perhaps a co-worker who feels threatened by the outburst, could take the exclamation personally and think it was directed at him, rather than wondering, "Is she angry with me, or just plain angry?"

a. COMMUNICATION STRESS

1. Self-assessment

The brief questionnaire on the next page will help you assess your current communication effectiveness. The higher your score (out of a total of 40) the better you communicate. If you score less than 25, you should work on your communication skills.

2. How we communicate

Imagine you're in the middle of an important discussion with someone. Perhaps you're buying a new suit or dress, arranging for a babysitter so you can go to a job interview, or exchanging views with a new friend.

Suddenly you can't hear anything. You see the other person's lips moving but you hear no sound. You can't say anything. You open your mouth to speak but no sound comes out. How do you feel?

This is a dramatic illustration of being unable to communicate. Thousands of us, every day, fail to communicate and we suffer stress reactions as a result. We miss important pieces of information; we speak, but fail to let the other person know exactly what we mean; we say no when we mean yes, or yes when we mean no. We feel and act confused, tense, and anxious because of unclear communication.

Communication — the structured transmission of meaning — takes place constantly. It occurs within us in the form of a running dialogue we call thinking. Our thoughts and our physical sensations are in constant communication, often without our awareness. As well, communication occurs between people as they speak, listen, and observe. What we say and how we say it are part of a continuous process of communication.

Every communication involves three parts: a *sender*, a *message*, and a *receiver*. The sender initiates the message; the message is the content and form of the communication; the receiver is the intended recipient of the message.

Stress management requires clear communication. When someone understands the message we have sent, providing we intend they understand it, we experience little stress. When we want to be understood but our efforts are unsuccessful, stress occurs. Imagine a child straining to be understood while struggling to master language, a stutterer trying to explain what he or she wants to purchase from an impatient store clerk, a diplomat who learns that a translator has just insulted the foreign minister of China. All such experiences produce acute stress.

Stress can also arise when we feel we have failed to communicate. Some people feel guilty for their failure to communicate love to a parent who has died. Some feel angry for days after they have suppressed feelings of anger. When such feelings persist for long periods of time, they become chronic and can be a factor in physical illness.

3. Touching and stress

You may have seen a popular bumper sticker with the message, "Have you hugged your kid today?" The question reminds us of the value of physical contact as nonverbal communication. A hug, for example, is an important way of conveying an "I love you" message.

During the nineteenth and early twentieth centuries, adults worried about spoiling children with physical displays of affection. Many infants died from a disease called *marasmus*, a Greek word that means "wasting away." In some orphanages near-

COMMUNICATION ASSESSMENT

Answer each question by circling the number that best describes the statement as it applies to you over the last month.

1 — Never true of me

2 — Rarely true of me

3 — More often true than false; frequently true of me

4 — Always true of me

	1	2	3	4
1. I like talking with other people in a one-to-one situation.	1	2	3	4
2. I like talking to small groups of people.	1	2	3	4
3. I like talking to a large audience of people.	1	2	3	4
4. I am not overly nervous when I have to talk to a group.	1	2	3	4
5. People tell me I am very easy to talk to.	1	2	3	4
6. People tell me their problems.	1	2	3	4
7. People listen to me when I talk.	1	2	3	4
8. I feel people understand me.	1	2	3	4
9. People tell me I communicate well.	1	2	3	4
10. I am able to get my ideas across clearly and simply.	1	2	3	4

TOTAL _____

ly all children died, not from poor nutrition or lack of medical care, but from a lack of physical contact. These infants simply had not been touched enough and they wasted away.

Touching is our first form of communication. Even before we are born the sensation of touch teaches us about our embryonic world. As we grow, our world expands. Our nervous system develops, stimulated through contact with our parents, particularly with our mother. The stress of infancy and childhood is managed through touch more effectively than any other way.

Have you hugged someone today? Has someone hugged you? Do you have some-one to touch? Young children have few inhibitions about asking to be hugged or cuddled, and they freely offer hugs and cuddles in return. Unfortunately, this spontaneity often decreases with age. In some cultures and for some people, a warm and caring touch is a frequent event; for others, it is rare. Many of us, particularly when under stress, do not admit our need for touching. Yet much stress in the work place, or between two people, can be eased with a pat on the back or a hug.

Which of the following touching activities did you experience last week? And, for the sake of stress management, decide which ones you will seek or avoid next week.

TOUCHING EXERCISE

TOUCH	LAST WEEK	NEXT WEEK
Hug		
Massage		
Physical fight		
Holding hands		
Dancing		
Stroking a pet		
Being in a crowded space		
Sexual contact		
Foot rub		
Back rub		
Other:		

b. INTERPERSONAL COMMUNICATION SKILLS

1. Verbal and nonverbal communication

Communication includes both spoken and unspoken messages. Researchers estimate that less than half the meaning of any message is conveyed verbally. Body posture, touch, gestures, tone of voice and, indeed, the arrangement of the physical environment, are often even more important than the words spoken.

Much is communicated by the words we use and the emphasis, or inflection, we give them. We also communicate in nonverbal ways such as frowning, crossing our arms, looking at the floor as we speak, blushing, looking at the clock, or beckoning with a hand. Some nonverbal behaviors convey an idea, such as putting a finger to your lips in a gesture of silence; others, such as smiling or pounding your fist on a desk, indicate feelings. These nonverbal signs and gestures are often different in different ethnic cultures. Misinterpreting such signs can lead to stress and culture shock.

Nonverbal behavior is often more spontaneous than words and can present a clearer meaning of what we intend to communicate. Therefore, nonverbal communication is a potential problem; we may think a person has closed his or her eyes out of boredom, when actually he or she closed them to concentrate better on what is being said. It's important to be sure we know the correct meaning of such behavior because it influences how we communicate.

Another possible problem can arise when *you are unaware that you are communicating messages nonverbally.* You may use many spontaneous nonverbal mannerisms, such as blinking, looking away, or rapping your fingers on furniture, as part of your personal style of communication. Some of these mannerisms have obvious meanings and may be correctly understood only by those who know you well, while they cause frequent confusion, misunderstanding, and stress for those who do not know you well.

It is important to become aware of your nonverbal mannerisms and to use them in

Less than half the meaning of any message is conveyed verbally

a way that matches what you are saying. You can then also help others learn what they mean as part of your personal, individual style of communicating.

For example, you might find it helpful to tell others, "People sometimes think I'm doubting them when they see me raise my eyebrows. That's generally not the case for me. I have a habit of raising my eyebrows when I hear something that especially interests me."

Here are four ways to improve your nonverbal communication:

(a) Look directly at the person to whom you are speaking to convey your genuine interest and attention.

(b) Face the person with whom you are speaking, and lean slightly toward him or her.

(c) Gesture appropriately with your hands. Your facial expressions should be consistent with your words. People sometimes smile when they are angry or joke when they have to say something unpleasant. Such forms of communication are basically dishonest and generate mistrust.

(d) Pay special attention to your level and tone of voice. A firm, even voice tone can be very effective in communicating assertiveness. A soft, pleasant voice tone communicates warmth and affection, whereas a whining, nasal voice tone can turn off the listener.

2. Feedback

Because we don't see ourselves, we are not always the best judges of how we are being perceived by others. To learn the truth, we sometimes need to go to an outside source for honest feedback. Feedback should be used to try to understand how you affect others. As in a guided missile system, feedback will help keep your behavior on target and, thus, better achieve your goals.

Feedback provides you with the opportunity to examine your own verbal and nonverbal communication patterns. The best way to get feedback is to have yourself videotaped. With the increasing popularity of videotape machines and cameras, you can rent one or borrow a friend's without difficulty. Have someone tape you and take time to watch yourself.

Another way to get feedback is to ask others to watch you and describe your behavior. You might ask a business colleague to watch you during a meeting and tell you afterward if there were any times that you appeared bored or overly aggressive, for example.

You can learn to watch for clues that may be communicating meanings nonverbally and causing you problems. If you suspect this is happening, it can sometimes help to suggest that the other person share his or her perception of how you are reacting.

Here are some criteria for useful feedback. In this discussion, the person who is responding to someone else's behavior and who is giving the feedback, is called the *giver*. The person whose behavior is being responded to, the one who is receiving the feedback, is called the receiver.

Useful feedback —

(a) is descriptive rather than evaluative. By describing the giver's own reaction, it leaves the receiver free to use or not use the feedback as it seems fit. By avoiding evaluative language, it reduces the receiver's need to react defensively.

(b) is specific rather than general. For the receiver to be told that he or she is dominating will probably not be as useful as to be told that "Just now when we were deciding the issue, you did not listen to what others said, and I felt forced to accept your arguments or face attack from you."

(c) takes into account the needs of both the receiver and the giver of feedback. Feedback can be destructive when it serves only the giver's needs and fails to consider the needs of the person on the receiving end.

(d) is directed toward behavior the receiver can do something about. Frustration is only increased when a person is reminded of some shortcoming over which he or she has no control.

(e) is solicited rather than imposed. Feedback is most useful when the receiver requests it.

(f) is well-timed. In general, feedback is most useful at the earliest opportunity after the given behavior, depending, of course, on the receiver's readiness to hear it, and the availability of support from others.

(g) is checked to insure clear communication. One way of doing this is to have the receiver try to rephrase the feedback received to see if it corresponds to what the sender has in mind.

(h) is verifiable. When feedback is given, both giver and receiver should have the opportunity to check with others the accuracy of the feedback. Is this one person's impression or an impression shared by others?

Feedback, then, is a corrective mechanism for the individual who wants to learn how well behavior matches intentions. It is a means for establishing identity — for answering, "Who am I?"

3. Active listening

Active listening helps you to be sure you understand the meaning of what another person is saying or doing. How do you check to make sure that you understand another person's ideas, information, or suggestions? How do you know that a remark means the same to you as it does to another?

You can, of course, get the other person to clarify the remark by asking, "What do you mean?" or, "Tell me more," or by saying, "I don't understand." After he or she has elaborated, however, you still face the same question, "Am I understanding the idea as it was intended to be understood?" Your feeling of certainty is no evidence that you do, in fact, understand.

Paraphrasing is a technique used to test and express our understanding. If you state in your own way what a remark conveys to you, the other person can determine whether the message is coming through as intended. Then, if you have misunderstood, the other person can speak directly to the specific misunderstanding you have revealed. The term *paraphrase* can be used for any means of showing the other person what an idea or suggestion means to you.

An additional benefit of paraphrasing is that it lets the other person know that you are interested. It is evidence that you want to understand what he or she means. If you can satisfy the other person that you really do understand, that person will probably be more willing to try to understand your views.

People sometimes think of active listening or paraphrasing as merely putting the other person's ideas in another way. They try to say the same thing with different words. Such word-swapping or parrotting may result merely in the *illusion* of mutual understanding, as in the following example:

Sarah: Jim should never have become a teacher.

Fred: You mean teaching isn't the right job for him?

Sarah: Exactly! Teaching is not the right job for Jim.

Fred still doesn't know why Sarah believes teaching isn't the right job for Jim. Instead of trying to record Sarah's statement, Fred might have asked himself, "What does Sarah's statement mean to me?" In that case the interchange might have sounded like this:

Sarah: Jim should never have become a teacher.

Fred: You mean he is too harsh on the children...maybe even cruel?

Sarah: Oh, no. I mean that he has such expensive tastes and he can't ever earn enough as a teacher.

Fred: Oh, I see. You think he should have gone into a field that would have insured him a higher standard of living?

Sarah: Exactly! Teaching is not the right job for Jim.

Effective paraphrasing is not a trick or a verbal gimmick. It comes from an attitude, a desire to know what the other means. And to satisfy this desire, you reveal the meaning a comment had for you so that the other person can check whether it matches the intended meaning.

If the other's statement is general, it may convey something *specific* to you:

Larry: I think this is a very poor textbook.

You: Poor? You mean it has too many inaccuracies?

Larry: No, the text is accurate, but the book comes apart too easily.

Possibly the other's comment suggests an *example* to you:

Laura: This text has too many omissions; we shouldn't adopt it.

You: Do you mean, for example, that it contains nothing about the role of native people in the development of the country?

Laura: Yes, that's one example. It also lacks any discussion of the development of the arts.

If the speaker's comment was very specific, it may convey a more *general* idea to you:

Ralph: Do you have 25 pencils I can borrow for my clients to use?

You: Do you just want something for them to write with? I have about 15 ball-point pens and 10 or 11 pencils.

Ralph: Great. Anything that writes will do.

Sometimes the other's idea will suggest its *inverse* or *opposite* meaning to you:

Stanley: I think the labor union acts so irresponsibly because management has ignored them so long.

You: Do you mean that the union would be less militant now if the bosses had consulted with them in the past?

Stanley: Certainly. I think the union is being forced to more and more desperate measures.

To develop your skill in understanding others, try different ways of conveying your interest in understanding what they mean and revealing what others' statements mean to you. Find out what kind of responses are helpful ways of paraphrasing for you.

The next time someone is angry with you, or is criticizing you, try to paraphrase until you can demonstrate that you understand what the other person is trying to convey. What effect does this have on your feelings and on the other person's feelings?

4. Miscommunication styles

Stress often results from communication styles that people have developed and practiced over many years in order to avoid dealing with feelings. Some of the most destructive of these stress-producing styles, which should be avoided, are described below:

(a) Avoiders

Avoiders refuse to fight. When a conflict arises, avoiders will leave, fall asleep, pretend to be busy at work, or keep from facing the problem in some other way. This behavior makes it very difficult for others to express feelings of anger or hurt because avoiders won't fight back. Arguing with an avoider is like trying to box with a person who won't even put up his or her gloves.

(b) Pseudoaccommodators

Not only do pseudoaccommodators refuse to face up to a conflict, they pretend there's nothing wrong. This really drives others, who definitely feel there's a problem, crazy and causes feelings of guilt and resentment toward the accommodator.

(c) Guilt makers

Instead of saying straight out that they don't want or approve of something, guilt makers try to change other people's behavior by making them feel responsible for causing pain. The guilt maker's favorite line is, "It's OK, don't worry about me...," accompanied by a big sigh.

(d) Subject changers

Really a type of avoider, subject changers escape facing aggression by shifting the conversation whenever it approaches an area of conflict. Because of these tactics, subject changers and their partners never have the chance to explore their problem and do something about it.

(e) Criticizers

Rather than come out and express their feelings of dissatisfaction, criticizers attack some other characteristic of their partner. Thus they never have to share what's really on their minds and can avoid dealing with the painful aspects of a relationship.

(f) Mindreaders

Instead of allowing others to honestly express their feelings, mindreaders go into character analysis, explaining what other people really mean or what is wrong with other people. By behaving this way, mindreaders refuse to handle their own feelings and leave no room for others to express themselves.

(g) Trappers

Trappers play dirty tricks by setting up desired behaviors for others, and then attacking the very thing requested. An example of this technique is for a trapper to say, "Let's be totally honest with each other," and then when the partner shares his or her feelings, the trapper attacks the partner for having feelings that the trapper doesn't want to accept.

(h) Crisis ticklers

Crisis ticklers never quite come out and express themselves. Instead of admitting concern about finances, for example, a crisis tickler innocently asks, "Gee, how much did that cost?" The crisis tickler drops an obvious hint but never really deals with a crisis!

(i) Gunnysackers

Gunnysackers don't respond immediately when angry. Instead, they put resentment into a gunnysack, which after a while begins to bulge with large and small gripes. Then, when the sack is about to burst, gunnysackers pour out all their pent-up aggression on the overwhelmed and unsuspecting victim.

(j) Trivial tyrannizers

Instead of honestly sharing resentment, trivial tyrannizers do things they know will annoy others: leaving dirty dishes in the sink, clipping fingernails in bed, belching out loud, turning up the television too loud, and so on.

(k) Jokers

Because jokers are afraid to face conflicts squarely, they kid around when others want to be serious, thus blocking the expression of important feelings.

(l) Beltliners

Everyone has a psychological beltline, and below it are subjects too sensitive to be approached without damaging a relationship. Beltlines may have to do with physical characteristics, intelligence, past behavior, or deeply ingrained personality traits a person is trying to overcome. In an attempt to get even or hurt someone, beltliners will use intimate knowledge to hit below the belt, where they know it will hurt.

(m) Blamers

Blamers are more interested in finding fault than in solving a conflict. Needless to say, they usually don't blame themselves. Blaming behavior almost never solves a conflict and is an almost sure-fire way to make the receiver defensive.

(n) Contract tyrannizers

Contract tyrannizers will not allow relationships to change. Whatever agreements the partners had about roles and responsibilities at one time, they'll remain unchanged. "It's your job to feed the baby, wash the dishes, and discipline the kids," and so on.

(o) Kitchen sink fighters

These people are so named because in an argument they bring up things that are totally off the subject: the way you behaved last New Year's Eve, the unbalanced checkbook, bad breath, everything but the kitchen sink.

(p) Withholders

Instead of expressing anger honestly and directly, withholders punish others by keeping back something — courtesy, affection, good cooking, humor, sex. As you can imagine, this is likely to build up even greater resentments in the relationship.

(q) Saboteurs

Saboteurs "get back" at others by failing to defend against attackers, and even by encouraging ridicule or disregard from outside the relationship.

c. ASSERTIVE COMMUNICATION

We live in an age of great turbulence. Many traditional values are being attacked or questioned. Amidst all the change, it's difficult to know how to behave or how to answer the question, "What is my opinion?"

The inability to answer such questions is, to many people, a cause of excessive stress. Their hesitancy, or incapacity to take a stand steadily erodes their self-esteem. That, in turn, makes them fear or avoid any sort of social encounter, and they become less and less competent to handle stress.

In this section you will examine *assertiveness* and learn how some simple techniques can help you overcome inhibitions and improve your ability to cope with stressful situations. You will first assess your assertiveness level. Then you will study what assertiveness is, and, equally important, what it is not. Finally, you will learn and practice some basic skills of assertiveness communication and re-assess your assertiveness level.

Naturally, only a brief overview of such a complex subject can be presented here. As an additional part of your program, therefore, we strongly recommend that you attend an assertiveness course or workshop, and read some of the books listed at the end of this chapter.

1. Assessing your assertiveness

Use the assertiveness checklist on the following page to assess your assertive skills.

Assertive people tend to have higher scores. The maximum possible is 88. If your score is above 60 you certainly don't need any help from us!

On the other hand, if your score is low, don't worry. The very fact that you are reading this book shows that you value

ASSERTIVENESS CHECKLIST

Use the following scale, circle the number that best applies to you.

1 — Never
2 — Occasionally
3 — Frequently
4 — Always

1. I tend to rely on my own judgment. 1 2 3 4
2. I have confidence in my own judgment. 1 2 3 4
3. I am aware of what I feel when I am feeling it. 1 2 3 4
4. I am honest with myself about what I want and feel. 1 2 3 4
5. I express what I feel when I feel it, regardless of other people. 1 2 3 4
6. I let others know what I am feeling about myself. 1 2 3 4
7. I let others know what I am feeling about them. 1 2 3 4
8. I am openly critical of others' ideas, opinions, and behavior
   if I disagree with them. 1 2 3 4
9. When a person is highly unfair I call it to his or her attention. 1 2 3 4
10. If I think there is a problem developing in a relationship, I let
    the other person know what I think. 1 2 3 4
11. I insist that my spouse or roommate take a fair share of
    household chores. 1 2 3 4
12. At work, if I think I am being asked to do more than I possibly
    can, I object. 1 2 3 4
13. If someone asks me a favor which is inconvenient for me to
    carry out, I tell them so. 1 2 3 4
14. If a person has borrowed something from me, a book,
    garment, or anything of value, and is overdue in returning it,
    I mention it to them. 1 2 3 4
15. I insist that my landlord, mechanic, or repairman make repairs,
    adjustments, or replacements that are his or her responsibility. 1 2 3 4
16. When I discover merchandise is faulty, I return it for an adjustment. . . . 1 2 3 4
17. I speak out in protest when someone takes my place in line. 1 2 3 4
18. When a latecomer is waited on before I am, I call attention to the
    situation. 1 2 3 4
19. If someone keeps kicking or bumping my chair in a movie or a lecture,
    I ask the person to stop. 1 2 3 4
20. In a restaurant, when my meal is improperly prepared or served,
    I ask the waiter or waitress to correct the situation. 1 2 3 4
21. When I need help, I ask for it. 1 2 3 4
22. When I am speaking, I object if someone interrupts. 1 2 3 4

TOTAL_____

72

yourself and are anxious to improve. A low score may simply indicate that you are being very honest with yourself.

2. What assertiveness is

The term *assertiveness* comes from an older usage, *self-assertiveness*. In one way the older form is preferable, meaning "the confident putting-forward of one's self, opinions, claims, or rights." Although we will continue to use the modern shorter form, it is worth keeping in mind the silent *self* — your self, you.

When we are assertive we let ourselves and other people know how we feel in an honest, firm, open manner. Assertiveness means that we take responsibility for our feelings and for letting people know how we feel. It also means that we respect ourselves, and we have equal respect for others.

Assertiveness is a normal form of behavior. Human beings have opinions, claims, and rights that affect other human beings, and sometimes, the only way that opinions can be heard, claims adjusted, and rights honored — the only way that justice can be done — is for individuals to put themselves forward and to assert those things to which they feel themselves entitled.

Assertive people are those who recognize their own needs and make these known to others clearly and confidently. Assertive people recognize that everybody else has exactly the same right to self-assertiveness as they do. They therefore assert their claims in a tactful manner and listen to the claims of others with respect.

Honesty is the hallmark of truly assertive people. They are addicted to reality and they tell things the way they see them without distortion or exaggeration. Truly assertive people seek knowledge, not illusions. They want to know who, in fact, they are, and who, in fact, other people are; they heed nothing else. They do not lie, because lies tell them nothing about themselves or others. Asserting your true self, not some imaginary self to con others, is the basis of self-assertiveness.

3. Is assertive behavior selfish?

Selfishness may be defined as a short-sighted preoccupation with one's own affairs, often to the complete exclusion of everyone else. As children, we learn that selfishness is bad and that others should come first.

Yet the degree to which one should care about others is a separate moral or philosophical issue from assertiveness. Assertiveness means recognizing and laying claim to our legitimate rights. If that is selfish then it is, on occasion, reasonable to be selfish. For instance, a mother of small children has a perfect right to rest from her child-care routines without being accused of selfishness. Often, in our efforts to avoid self-indulgence, we develop patterns of self-denial that are more harmful than selfishness. In order to avoid the selfish label, we not only put the needs of other people ahead of our own, we also sacrifice our integrity and self-respect, even when our desires are perfectly legitimate.

It may turn out that if you don't take care of yourself, you won't be able to take care of others, no matter how much you want to do so.

4. What assertiveness is not

Assertiveness implies honesty and respect for the rights of others. Non-assertiveness or false-assertiveness, on the other hand, usually involves either dishonesty, lack of respect for others, or both, as in manipulation.

People who are unwilling or afraid to assert themselves often resort to other means to get what they want. For instance, one or the other partner in a marriage may want a new car but be unwilling to address the subject directly because of anticipated opposition to the expense involved. He or she will, instead, keep a constant barrage of complaints about the existing vehicle. Eventually, the other partner can't stand it, and makes the forbidden suggestion, "Maybe we ought to buy a new car." Contrast these tactics with the assertive, honest, respectful, "Honey, I think we need a new car, even though it's expensive. What do you think?"

Sometimes, dropping hints can be quite innocent or playful. It becomes serious, however, when an individual sees other people as opponents to be outwitted. Such an attitude works when playing chess or fighting wars, but is totally inappropriate in relationships or other social interactions.

People can be manipulated in many ways; we will discuss only some of the most common. As you read, ask yourself two questions, "Am I aware that I have been manipulated in some of these ways? Do I use these dirty tricks to manipulate others?" Remember, all these situations are two-way streets.

(a) Aggressiveness or intimidation

Probably the most common form of false assertiveness is aggressiveness, which is often a cover-up of inner uncertainty more than an excess of assertiveness. Assertiveness and aggressiveness belong on two completely different scales, so a person who becomes more assertive is in no real danger of becoming extremely aggressive.

People with a fair measure of self-esteem and who are not basically timid, may resort to aggressiveness on occasion to achieve some end. An employer, for example, may explode in anger when he or she wants greater productivity. Another example might be a mother in a basically happy family who uses anger to try and frighten her children into doing what she wants. Sudden outbursts of anger are shocking or intimidating to most of us.

Such behavior is not necessary. Open, honest, and direct communication of the individual's needs is more likely to earn respect and achieve desired results. You can choose to relate, or to alienate.

(b) Helplessness

Helplessness is the opposite of aggressiveness. Instead of appealing to our fears with aggressive behavior underlaid with threats of violence, the helpless individual appeals to our goodwill, sympathy, or pity.

Some people feel that social status, age, or condition entitles them to extra respect or services. Others are afraid of being nuisances and so will ask for help only indirectly. Whatever their motivation, instead of making direct, straightforward requests, these people have learned to rely on frequent appeals such as "Help me, I can't," to satisfy their needs. This behavior eventually results in increased loss of self-esteem.

An elderly lady might communicate her loneliness indirectly by saying, "I used to have a dog but I can't get around to feed one now. I loved talking to Bozo." She could instead communicate directly, "I am very lonely. Could you spare an hour to chat once in a while?"

Other examples of using helplessness to manipulate others include a boss who claims that without help she will go bankrupt, a patient insisting that without her doctor she will die, a spouse or lover who says that he can't manage without you.

With the exception of babies, most people can handle daily life. Remember this whenever someone says, "I can't."

(c) Guilt

The manipulator may seek to inspire guilt to force someone to behave in a certain way. This form of manipulation often includes the accusation of selfishness or the brandishing of duties or obligations.

A man who needs help building a garage may, instead of simply asking for help, remind his neighbor of past favors: loaning a snowblower, helping fix the roof, and looking after children. He is maintaining that, because he has helped his neighbor, the neighbor is obligated to help in return. This is not the case. One good turn may deserve another, but no obligation exists to return favors.

In another case, a mother may be tired and want help with some chores. Instead of asking for it outright, she reminds her children of all she has done for them and makes them feel that they will be bad, ungrateful, and selfish if they do not help.

The use of guilt is sometimes almost a habit in some relationships. Frequently, refusals are greeted with, "Don't you love me any more?"

(d) Criticism

Criticism of behavior can be a form of manipulation. In this case, the object of the critic is to put the other person on the defensive, drawing attention away from the critic, rather than to offer constructive advice. Be cautious in judging criticism, however. In many cases it is simply an honest assertion by another, and your defensiveness may indicate your lack of assertiveness. All criticism should be carefully considered, to see if there isn't some truth from which we can benefit. If we don't feel like receiving criticism at a particular time, we can say so and defer it.

(e) Teasing

Teasing is often related to uncalled-for criticism. The intent of the teaser may be to deflect attention from himself or herself. Teasing is, however, most commonly used as a means of indirect persuasion, to shame or ridicule someone into doing things he or she doesn't want to do. An example might be an adolescent boy teased by his peers for being chicken if he does not use drugs or take part in some risky, and possibly foolish, enterprise.

Teasing can, however, be done in a friendly, gentle, or loving manner, and not necessarily be manipulative. Chiding a loved one for a foolish act may be the best way of preventing repetition of the mistake.

(f) Questioning our motives

We should be wary of questions about our actions that start with why. The questioner may wish to criticize our decisions or our motivation, but lack the courage to do so directly. Or he or she may feel entitled to an apology and be trying to make us feel apologetic. Wariness is all that is needed. If we make mistakes, there may be a need to apologize. On the other hand, mistakes are perfectly natural; nobody is infallible.

5. Are you an assertive communicator?

The chart on the following page compares passive, assertive, and aggressive behaviors. Read the comparison and circle any items that describe you. Are you more often assertive, aggressive, or passive?

In developing assertiveness it is helpful to have a set of guidelines for daily practice. The greater the degree to which you can follow these guidelines, the more helpful they will be.

Use the checklist on page 77 to see if you live by assertive guidelines. The assertive communicator would answer Yes rather than No to each question. What do you do?

Dedicate yourself to working on problem areas revealed in this exercise. After a few weeks, review the checklists and see if you have overcome the problem. This may take time to achieve, so don't worry if you seem slow. Just keep at it!

ASSERTIVENESS CHARACTERISTICS

	PASSIVE	ASSERTIVE	AGGRESSIVE
CHARACTERISTICS	Allow others to choose for you. Emotionally dishonest. Indirect, self-denying, inhibited. In win-lose situations you lose. If you do get your own way, it is indirectly.	Choose for self. Tactfully honest. Direct, self-respecting, self-expressing, straightforward. Convert win-lose to win-win.	Choose for others. Tactlessly honest. Direct, self-enhancing. Self-expressive, derogatory. In win-lose situation, you win.
FEELINGS IN THE EXCHANGE	Anxious, ignored, helpless, manipulated. Later: angry at yourself and/or others.	Confident, self-respecting, goal oriented, valued. Later: accomplished.	Righteous, superior, deprecatory, controlling. Later: possibly guilty.
OTHERS' FEELINGS IN THE EXCHANGE	Guilty or superior. Frustrated with you.	Valued, respected.	Humiliated, defensive, resentful, hurt.
OTHERS' VIEW OF YOU IN THE EXCHANGE	Lack of respect. Distrust. A push-over. Do not know where you stand.	Respect, trust, know where you stand.	Vengeful, angry, distrustful, fearful.
OUTCOME	Others achieve their goals at your expense. Your rights are violated.	Outcome determined by above-board negotiation. Your and others' rights respected.	You achieve your goal at others' expense. Your rights upheld; others' rights violated.
UNDERLYING BELIEF SYSTEM	I should never make anyone uncomfortable or displeased ...except myself.	I have a responsibility to protect my own rights; I respect others but not necessarily their behavior.	I have to put others down to protect myself.

ASSERTIVENESS CHECKLIST

When I talk to someone, I..

	Yes	No
— am polite, but firm; I avoid apologizing.	☐	☐
— use "I" instead of "it."	☐	☐
— am direct and to the point; I avoid long explanations.	☐	☐
— usually start off by saying no if I want to refuse a request.	☐	☐
— anticipate feelings in close relationships; I acknowledge the other's feelings.	☐	☐
— seek mutually acceptable compromises.	☐	☐
— use a volume appropriate to the circumstances, not too loud or too soft.	☐	☐
— use a firm voice, indicating that I am firm.	☐	☐
— use a lively intonation of voice to convey ease.	☐	☐
— respond quickly and without hesitation to show I know what I want.	☐	☐
— speak in a clear voice to get my message across.	☐	☐
— speak fluently, without ahs and uhms, which indicate uncertainty.	☐	☐
— look directly at the other person.	☐	☐
— am sincere — no unnecessary smiles, grimaces, biting lips, and so on.	☐	☐
— try to keep my hands, arms, and legs relaxed.	☐	☐
— avoid sitting stiffly, I convey ease.	☐	☐

CHAPTER 6 READING LIST

Alberti, R.E. and Emmons, M.L. *Your Perfect Right: A Guide to Assertive Living*. San Luis Obispo, California: Impact Publications California, 1982.

Bach, G. and Goldberg H. *Creative Aggression: The Art of Assertive Living*. New York: Doubleday, 1983.

Bower, G. and Bower, S. *Asserting Yourself*. Reading, Massachusetts: Addison-Wesley, 1976.

Cawood, D. *Assertiveness for Managers*. North Vancouver, British Columbia: Self-Counsel Press, 1988.

Hall, E.T. *The Hidden Dimension*. New York: Doubleday, 1966.

Knapp, M.L. *Nonverbal Communication in Human Interaction*. New York: Holt, 1978.

McKay, M. and Davis, M. *Messages: The Communication Book*. Oakland, California: New Harbinger Publications, 1983.

Mehrabian, A. *Nonverbal Communication*. Hawthorne, New York: Aldine Publishing, 1972.

Montagu, A. *Touching: The Human Significance of Skin*. New York: Harper & Row, 1978.

Osborn, S.M. and Harris, G.G. *Assertive Training for Women*. Springfield, Illinois: Charles C. Thomas, 1978.

Phelps, Stanlee, and Austin, N. *The Assertive Woman*. San Luis Obispo, California: Impact Publications California, 1975.

Proshansky, H.M., et al. *Environmental Psychology: People and Their Physical Setting*. New York: Holt Rinehart & Winston, 1976.

Sommer, R. *Design Awareness*. San Francisco: Rinehart Press, 1972.

_____. *Personal Space: The Behavioral Basis of Design*. Englewood Cliffs, New Jersey: Prentice-Hall, 1969.

Zimbardo, P.G. *Shyness: What It is, What To Do About It*. New York: Addison-Wesley, 1977.

7
YOUR GENERAL HEALTH AND WELL-BEING

Sound health habits and a sense of well-being are the foundation of effective stress management. In this chapter, we review the basics of good nutrition, exercise, sleep habits, and the development of social support systems from the holistic view of physical, mental and spiritual harmony. Our intention is to help you become aware of how well, or how badly, you are looking after yourself.

You may learn some new ideas for self-care in these pages, or discover that you know the basics, but have neglected certain important health practices. In preventive medicine, we have found that it is better to know a little and apply all you know than to know a lot and apply little. Some people, for example, concentrate on good nutrition but ignore their need for rest and physical exercise, while others focus on exercise and neglect the other important aspects of health.

This chapter is divided into five major parts: exercise, nutrition, harmful habits, building supportive relationships, and rest. In each part, we review the basic information by which you can measure your present level of practice in that aspect of general health. This form of self-assessment is an important first step in your personal preventive medicine program.

a. EXERCISE

Physical fitness contibutes to good health and a long life, improves the quality of life, and assists in achieving a state of relaxation. Recent studies have shown that physical exercise is a valuable part of treatment for depression and helps to improve intellectual capacity. Also, increased physical activity can burn off excess calories and decrease obesity.

Our approach to total physical fitness is based on the five S's: safety, suppleness, stamina, strength, and satisfaction.

1. Safety

Many people think the way to get the most out of exercising is to stretch and strain until they are sore all over. This theory is dangerous. The following guidelines will help you avoid injuries:

(a) The first step is to complete the Physical Activity Readiness Questionnaire (Par-Q) on the following page. This self-administered test is a sensible first step if you are planning to increase the amount of physical activity in your life. The results will indicate if you are ready to begin your exercise program.

(b) Learn about the sport or activity you intend to try. Talk with friends about the sports you are interested in; get background information to find a suitable activity.

(c) Do strengthening exercises prior to beginning a new sport. Concentrate on areas most susceptible to injury.

(d) Go slowly. The older you are, the more slowly you should start. Move up very gradually, even if it takes six months to get to a level with which you are satisfied. Start off by doing half of what you think you can do.

(e) Minimize competition. If you want to compete, find someone your own level, otherwise you will try to do too much or strain yourself by competing against someone working at a level higher than your own.

(f) Always warm up prior to any sporting activity.

(g) Take at least five minutes to cool down after any activity by stretching or walking slowly.

2. Suppleness

Suppleness is the opposite of rigidity. Suppleness, or flexibility, contributes to a general muscular relaxation throughout the body and is helpful in reducing the harmful effects of stress. Well-developed suppleness also prevents damage to the body from sudden exertion.

PHYSICAL ACTIVITY READINESS QUESTIONNAIRE (PAR-Q)*

For most people physical activity should not pose any problem or hazard. Par-Q has been designed to identify the small number of adults for whom physical activity might be unwise, or who should have medical advice concerning the type of activity most suitable for them.

Common sense is your best guide to answering these few questions. Read them carefully and check the appropriate box.

	YES	NO
1. Has your doctor ever said you have heart trouble?	☐	☐
2. Do you frequently have pains in your heart and chest?	☐	☐
3. Do you often feel faint or have spells or severe dizziness?	☐	☐
4. Has a doctor ever said your blood pressure was too high?	☐	☐
5. Has your doctor ever told you that you have a bone or joint problem such as arthritis that has been aggravated by exercise?	☐	☐
6. Are you over age 65 and not accustomed to vigorous exercise?	☐	☐
7. Is there a good physical reason not mentioned here why you should not follow an activity program even if you wanted to?	☐	☐

• If you answered YES to one or more questions—

If you have not recently done so, consult with your personal physician by telephone or in person before increasing your physical activity or taking a fitness test. Tell your doctor what questions you answered "yes" on Par-Q, or show him or her your copy.

After medical evaluation, ask your doctor for advice about your suitability for unrestricted physical activity, probably on a gradually increasing basis, or restricted or supervised activity to meet your specific needs, at least on an initial basis.

Check in your community for special programs or services.

• If you answered NO to all questions—

You can begin a graduated exercise program. A gradual increase in proper exercise promotes good fitness development while minimizing or eliminating discomfort.

You can also take part in an exercise test if you desire. Fitness tests are available at many fitness centres, YM/YWCAs, or community centers.

*Produced by the British Columbia Ministry of Health and the Department of National Health and Welfare.

You can develop suppleness by stretching certain muscle groups. When you practice stretching, however, it is important to learn to relax muscles so that they can be stretched fully.

There are three types of stretches: the easy stretch, the developmental stretch, and the drastic stretch.

The easy stretch is accomplished while you are totally relaxed. The developmental stretch is more intense, and goes almost to the level of discomfort. The drastic stretch can be painful, and should not be attempted. The length of your stretch will gradually increase using the easy and developmental stretches.

Stretching is particularly important when warming up for aerobic exercises, such as handball or cross-country skiing. It is also useful by itself, and can assist in decreasing arthritic problems. The following guidelines should be followed when you begin stretching exercises.

(a) Pay attention to the stretch, not your flexibility.

(b) Try to avoid competition or comparison with others.

(c) Focus on the feeling of relaxation in the stretch.

(d) Be aware of your breathing. Allow it to become slow and rhythmical, helping you make a relaxed stetch.

(e) Do not hold your breath while stretching.

(f) When stretching, focus on the area being stretched. Imagine yourself breathing through that area.

(g) Stretch within your limits.

(h) Do not bounce. This may lead to a drastic stretch, and cause injury!

For further details see the book, *Stretching* by Bob Anderson, or *Bend and Stretch* by Gord Stewart and Bob Faulkner, referred to in the reading list at the end of the chapter.

3. Stamina

Your stamina, or aerobic fitness, is your body's ability to make the most use of the oxygen you breathe. When you are aerobically fit, you are able to use oxygen more quickly, giving you more energy. Your heart and lungs also function at a higher level. Simply put, you can run faster and for longer periods of time.

There are four basic requirements for becoming aerobically fit.

(a) Frequency

Exercise four times a week.

(b) Intensity

Exercise vigorously, but not too vigorously. You can establish your own rate of exercising by trying the "talk test," which means that you are able to continue talking in a reasonable manner while exercising. Your pulse rate is another indication. To discover what your *training pulse rate* should be, subtract your age from 200 and then subtract your age from 170. The two answers give you the range of heart beats per minute you should work toward. For example, if you are 30 years old, your training pulse rate should be between 170 beats per minute (200-30), and 140 beats per minute (170-30). Table #2 shows the suggested ranges for various ages.

(c) Time

Exercise for 15 to 20 minutes each time.

(d) Type

Do exercises that can be done continuously; this means tennis, which stops and starts, will not give you the same degree of aerobic training as something like jogging, cycling, or swimming. You should also be using large muscle groups simultaneously such as arms, legs, chest, and trunk muscles.

Aerobic exercises also help fight stress by relaxing your state of mind. Jogging and cycling, for example, tend to free our minds from worry. With practice, we learn to use

TABLE #2
SUGGESTED PULSE RATES WHILE EXERCISING

Age	Pulse rate
20	150 — 180
25	145 — 175
30	140 — 170
35	135 — 165
40	130 — 160
45	125 — 155
50	120 — 150
55	115 — 145
60	110 — 140

only the muscles required for the exercise, leaving the others relaxed and comfortable. Long-distance runners, for instance, keep all muscles not being used in a relaxed state, thus conserving energy for the task at hand.

4. Strength

The stronger your body, the more able you are to deal with physical demands. Strengthening exercises can also help you maintain a well-proportioned body and prepare you for sudden demands, such as moving furniture. They are particularly important in preparing for certain sports, such as skiing, where you want to build up particular muscles.

Seek out a strengthening program that suits you personally, taking into consideration your age, stature, and any medical problems. It is important to note that strength-building exercises may not give you aerobic fitness, even though there is usually some overlap of benefits from these two types of exercises. Strength is increased by doing greater amounts of work for shorter periods of time as compared to aerobic fitness, which is achieved by doing lesser amounts of work for longer periods of time. Many community centers, YM/YWCAs, and other organizations offer fitness programs with a good strengthening component.

Table #3 gives you a general idea of the type of exercise you are getting.

Note that participating in one sport does not guarantee sufficient flexibility or strength. Also, some sports give aerobic exercise only if done continuously and with moderate vigor. Therefore, best results are obtained from participating in a variety of sports or by doing activities specifically designed for each type, that is, stretching for flexibility, jogging for aerobics, and weight lifting for strength.

Once you begin a program, record your daily amounts of exercise for one week on the exercise chart on page 84, placing a check mark in the appropriate box. We suggest you do 10 minutes of flexibility exercises 4 times weekly, 15 to 20 minutes of aerobic exercise 4 times weekly, and strengthening exercises 3 times weekly. Use the list of activities in Table #3 to help you determine what type of exercise you are getting from each activity. For each day write the type of exercise and number of minutes. Put check marks to indicate if you remembered to warm up and cool down.

TABLE #3
ACTIVITY EVALUATION

	STAMINA (Aerobics)	SUPPLENESS*	STRENGTH
BADMINTON		X	X
BALLET		X	X
BASKETBALL	X	X	X
BICYCLING	X		X
BOWLING		X	X
CALISTHENICS		X	X
CROSS-COUNTRY SKIING	X	X	X
DANCING		X	X
FOOTBALL			X
GOLF		X	
GYMNASTICS		X	X
HANDBALL	X	X	X
HOCKEY	X	X	X
JOGGING	X		
RUGBY	X	X	X
SKATING	X		X
SKIING (DOWNHILL)		X	X
SOFTBALL		X	X
SOCCER	X	X	X
SQUASH OR RACQUETBALL	X	X	
STAIR CLIMBING			X
SWIMMING	X	X	X
TENNIS		X	X
VOLLEYBALL		X	X
WALKING QUICKLY	X		
WEIGHT LIFTING			X
YOGA		X	

* Most exercises provide stretching for only part of the body. Full benefit will be enhanced by formal stretching exercises. Also, note that some exercises done continuously (e.g., calisthenics and dancing), would provide stamina training.

EXERCISE CHART

	Day 1	Day 2	Day 3	Day 4	Day 5	Day 6	Day 7
Warm up?							
Stamina (aerobics) Type: Minutes:							
Suppleness (flexibility) Type: Minutes:							
Strengthening Type: Minutes:							
Cool down?							

Note: You may list some exercises in all three categories. For example, if you played racquetball continuously for 30 minutes, it could be entered in all 3 categories for the day.

Pin the chart up where you and your family or friends can see it. This will help remind you, as well as provide social support. You can also record other aspects of your fitness training such as your pulse rate, your time over a certain distance, your flexibility, your weight, your body measurements, and so on. All this data provides encouraging feedback. Note that in some cases, exercising will not help reduce weight. You may become thinner, because the weight transfers itself from your fat to your muscles, but you may not become any lighter.

If, after two weeks, you wish to upgrade your fitness training, we suggest you read one or two of the books in the reading list at the end of this chapter. These will provide you with guidance and specifics on establishing a more advanced exercise program.

5. Satisfaction

Exercise ought to be an activity you enjoy. There are so many types of exercise and sports to choose from that boredom is almost inexcusable. Yet, some people do find exercise boring and give it up. If they have become used to being inactive, the effort to exercise may seem tedious at first.

One solution is to become involved with other people who are active and make exercise an integral part of your business, social, and recreation life. This way, you are exercising and developing social supports at the same time. Join two friends for a morning jog that takes place on schedule. With two friends sharing your jog, one can be away and you still have a friend for your morning exercise.

You can also —

- join a fitness group

- discuss business during a walk rather than over dinner
- socialize while skating rather than eating
- invite a friend on a canoe trip
- take a backpacking or cycling holiday
- coach a young team and take part in the exercise

Discontinue any exercise activity you don't enjoy. If you don't like jogging, take up hiking, swimming, or some other activity you would enjoy more.

Make it convenient to do your exercises at home. Try doing them in your bedroom. Put a stretch chart on your wall, or have a skipping rope available. Have your exercise clothing laid out and handy to put on when you wake up in the morning.

Invent ways to make your routine exercises more enjoyable. Listen to music on headphones, watch the news on TV, or dance to your favorite music. Anything goes!

b. NUTRITION

We have the opportunity today to eat better, be healthier, and enjoy our food more than any previous generation. Modern technology has made an unparalleled abundance of food available to us in North America, challenging our ability to choose wisely.

Yet it is easy to get caught up in the controversies of nutrition. Many popular diet plans, for instance, are products of personal bias or are not based on scientific evidence. There is also the controversy about the relationship between cholesterol and heart disease and the controversy about various foods that may be carcinogens. Consequently, people often feel confused about what to do about their diets.

We have chosen, therefore, to give you the basic guidelines of nutrition. Applying these basics will ensure that your eating is balanced, healthy, nutritious, and enjoyable.

Invite a friend on a canoe trip

Enjoyable is a key word in healthy eating. With a little care, every meal can be a pleasure. Try to make eating a sociable, happy time, as people used to do when life was less hurried. To keep mealtime relaxed, save problems for discussion at some other time. They will probably wait and you, having enjoyed a good meal, will be in a better state of mind to deal with them afterwards.

Eating is one of life's great pleasures. By all means, enjoy! By employing the basics, you can eat confidently, knowing that it will give you good health as well as pleasure.

1. Nutrition basics

There are six basic guidelines to good nutrition:

(a) Follow the Food Guide.

(b) Have ample amounts of unrefined food.

(c) Keep processing of food to a minimum.

(d) Keep fat intake to less than 35%.

(e) Avoid excessive salt.

(f) Drink plenty of fluids.

(a) Follow the Food Guide

The Food Guide divides foods into four basic groups. Each group emphasizes a particular range of essential nutrients. To assure a well-balanced diet, you should eat food from each of the groups every day. Table #4 shows recommended daily intakes.

Take calcium as an example. The recommended daily intake of calcium can be obtained by consuming foods in the milk products group, but it would be difficult to obtain from the other groups. By contrast, folic acid and vitamin C can be obtained from the fruit and vegetable group, but not so well from milk products or the other groups. If you follow the recommended servings in the Food Guide, you will be guaranteed adequate amounts of the basic nutrients, including fats, carbohydrates, proteins, vitamins, and minerals.

Study the Food Guide carefully. It is so simple that its principles can be absorbed in a couple of readings and remembered for daily use thereafter.

Table #5 shows the nutrients found in the different food groups and how each nutrient contributes to your well-being.

(b) Have ample amounts of unrefined foods

(i) Whole foods

When food is refined, part of the whole is removed. In refining whole wheat, for instance, bran and wheat germ are removed from the grain. Likewise, apple juice is an apple with the fibre removed, and olive oil is only part of the original olive.

When food is processed, however, either whole or refined food is mechanically modified by grinding, breaking, or heating. Therefore, whole grain flour is a processed food, but the whole, unrefined wheat kernel has been ground into flour. While flour is both refined and processed: something has been removed from the grain, and it has been ground as well.

Some interesting experiments have explored what happens in our bodies when we eat whole, refined, or processed foods. Volunteers were fed apples (whole food), blended apples (processed food), and apple juice (refined food). After the feeding, the blood sugars of the three volunteer groups were different, and the insulin put out by the pancreas was different. The results of the test are illustrated on the chart on page 89. The whole apple produces smaller changes in blood sugar. The demand on the pancreas (the gland that produces insulin) is also less for the apple than for both the puree or apple juice. It has been suggested that eating whole foods makes us less prone to developing diabetes. Problems caused by low blood

Eat a variety of foods from each group every day

Energy needs vary with age, sex and activity. Foods selected according to the guide can supply 1,000 to 1,400 calories. For additional energy, increase the number and size of servings from the various food groups and add other foods, but maintain a balance from this guide. Too much of one food can decrease absorption of other nutrients. For example, iron is absorbed better if vitamin C is present.

Milk and milk products

Children up to 11 years — 2-3 servings
Adolescents — 3-4 servings
Pregnant and nursing women — 3-4 servings
Adults — 3-4 servings
Skim, 2%, whole, buttermilk, reconstituted dry or evaporated milk may be used as a beverage or as the main ingredient in other foods. Cheese may also be chosen.
Examples of one serving
250 mL (1 cup) milk, yogurt or cottage cheese
45 g (1½ ounces) cheddar or process cheese
In addition, a supplement of vitamin D is recommended when milk is consumed which does not contain added vitamin D.

Meat and alternates

2 servings
Examples of one serving
60 to 90 g (2-3 ounces) cooked lean meat, poultry, liver or fish
60 mL (4 tablespoons) peanut butter
250 mL (1 cup) cooked dried peas, beans or lentils
80 to 250 mL (⅓-1 cup) nuts or seeds
60 g (2 ounces) cheddar, process, or cottage cheese
2 eggs

Bread and cereals

3-5 servings
whole grain or enriched. Whole grain products are recommended.
Examples of one serving
1 slice bread
125 to 250 mL (½-1 cup) cooked or ready-to-eat cereal
1 roll or muffin
125 to 250 mL (½-¾ cup) cooked rice, macaroni, spaghetti

Fruits and vegetables

4-5 servings
Include at least two vegetables.
Choose a variety of both vegetables and fruits — cooked, raw or their juices. Include yellow or green or green leafy vegetables.
Examples of one serving
125 mL (½ cup) vegetables or fruits
125 mL (½ cup) juice
1 medium potato, carrot, tomato, peach, apple, orange, or banana

TABLE #5
MAIN NUTRIENTS CONTRIBUTED BY THE FOOD GROUPS

Nutrient	Major functions	Milk and milk products	Bread and cereals	Fruits and vegetables	Meat and alternates
Carbohydrate	Supplies energy Assists in the utilization of fats Spares protein		X	X	
Fat	Supplies energy Aids in the absorption of fat soluble vitamins	X			X
Protein	Builds and repairs body tissues Builds antibodies to fight infection	X	X		X
Vitamin A	Aids normal bone and tooth development Maintains the health of the skin and lining membranes Permits good night vision	X		X	X
Thiamin	Releases energy from carbohydrates Aids normal growth and appetite Maintains normal function of the nervous system and gastrointestinal tract		X	X	X
Riboflavin	Maintains healthy skin and eyes Maintains a normal nervous system Releases energy to body cells during metabolism	X	X		X
Niacin	Aids normal growth and development Maintains normal function of the nervous system and gastrointestinal tract		X		X
Folic acid	Aids red blood cell formation			X	X
Vitamin C	Maintains healthy teeth and gums Maintains strong blood vessel walls			X	
Vitamin D	Enhances calcium and phosphorus utilization in the formation and maintenance of healthy bones and teeth	X			
Calcium	Aids in the formation and maintenance of strong bones and teeth Permits healthy nerve function and normal blood clotting	X			
Iron	An essential part of hemoglobin, the red blood cell constituent that transports oxygen and carbon dioxide		X	X	X

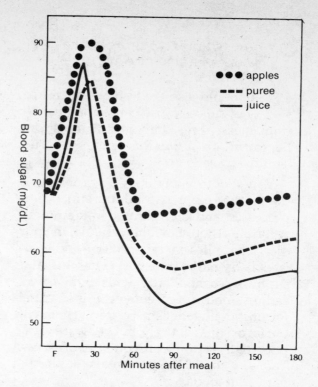

Mean blood/sugar levels in nine normal subjects after eating 60 grams of carbohydrate as whole apples, apple puree, and apple juice.

sugar, are also improved by eating whole, unrefined foods and unprocessed foods.

(ii) Fibre

Fibre assists in the process of digestion, and we need adequate fibre on a daily basis. Lack of fibre has been associated with a number of problems including constipation, hemorrhoids, cancer of the bowel, and diabetes.

This is why whole wheat bread is preferable to white bread, and whole wheat flour to white flour. Naturally, you would not make a white cake with pumpernickel flour, but you should be aware that fibre is missing from white flour. If you eat products made from white flour, be sure to obtain fibre from other sources.

(iii) Empty calorie foods

One of the popular villains in the field of nutrition is so-called junk or empty calorie food — food which is high in calories but low in nutrients. The bad reputation of cookies and candy, chips, soft drinks, ice cream, and other snacks and beverages is well deserved; they are full of sugar and fat and they satisfy hunger without satisfying bodily needs. Carefully monitor the frequency and amount of your intake of such foods. They lack real food value and mindless consumption of these is one of the leading causes of excess body weight.

Some people cut out white sugar in favor of honey or brown sugar. Unfortunately, this will not change much, except the taste of your coffee! Brown or raw sugar has no significant nutritional value and is no better or worse than white sugar. The same is true of honey. Most nutritionists agree, as a general policy, that sugar — be it white, brown, or honey –– should be cut down, and particularly so if you wish to lose weight.

Food and drink that are high in sugar also tend to adhere to the teeth and are a major contributing factor of tooth decay. Always brush your teeth after eating, before bed, and first thing in the morning.

(c) Keep processing to a minimum

Food preparation can diminish the nutritional value of certain foods. Deep frying, for example, sharply reduces the nutritional value of potatoes. Boiling vegetables leaches out water soluble vitamins and minerals. High heat also tends to damage protein. Some breakfast cereals are damaged in this way and should not be used as substitutes for whole grain products.

Also food stored over a long time loses nutritional value. Potatoes, for instance, have lost much of their vitamin C by the end of the winter. Ideally, food should be eaten fresh and with as little cooking as is feasible. So, steam your vegetables, or use little water, and keep the water to make sauces.

(d) Keep fat to less than 35%

Excessive fat intake is another major contributor to overweight. In our meat-eating culture, we consume large amounts of fat along with our steaks, lamb chops, pork roasts, and bacon. Fat has more than twice as many calories as carbohydrates. This high calorie meat consumption, added to a sedentary lifestyle, makes it all too easy to become overweight.

Most North Americans consume 40% to 45% of their food intake in fats. For the sake of your health, try to keep your fat consumption below 35%. Trim off as much fat as you can when you eat meat, and try to switch to a more varied diet that includes plenty of fish, which is lower in fat content.

Many people do not realize that steaks, weiners, and cheese are high in fat and calories. On the other hand, they avoid eating bread, because they believe it is high in calories. It may surprise you to consider the following calorie comparisons —

- A 6-ounce sirloin steak has 636 calories, while 8 slices of whole wheat bread add up to only 576 calories.

- A 1-inch cube of cheddar cheese has 70 calories, only 2 less than a slice of whole wheat bread, which has 72 calories.

- One weiner (2 ounces) has 170 calories, an amount equal to 2¼ slices of bread.

You should also try to have fat from a variety of sources. You can get animal fat from cheese, eggs, and meat. Plant fat can be found in avocados, peanuts, and sunflower seeds.

You should experience no problems if the fat you eat is natural, unrefined, unprocessed, and kept to a moderate amount. A certain amount of fat is essential in your diet. It supplies energy, protects and insulates body parts, transports vitamins, and supplies essential fatty acids. Similarly, a certain amount of carbohydrate is essential for proper metabolism. So don't try to cut out fat or sugar entirely, but be aware of the potentially serious consequences of excess. Table #6 shows the percentage of fat in a variety of foods.

(e) Avoid excessive salt

Most authorities agree that if you are prone to hypertension, salt can make the condition worse. Therefore, as a basic formula, we suggest cutting by half the amount of salt called for in any recipe, and that you stop sprinkling salt on your food.

After cutting down on salt for awhile, your tastes will adapt and seemingly bland food will taste good, while salted food will become unpleasant. Salting largely is a question of habit and custom. It is not essential.

Exceptions to this rule are people who are exposed to hot climates, summer warm spells, or are engaged in heavy, prolonged work or sport. If you fit this category, you require slightly more salt. This can be achieved with *light* salting of food. For most of us, the salt required in our diet is obtained readily in meat and other prepared foods, such as bread.

(f) Drink plenty of fluids

Adequate fluid intake is necessary for digestion, regulating body temperature,

90

transporting nutrients, and for proper kidney function. Most fluid requirements can be obtained from plain water, fruits, and vegetables. Be careful not to rely on obtaining most of your fluids through coffee, tea, soft drinks, or alcoholic beverages, as you may be acquiring too much caffeine, sugar, or alcohol.

2. Vitamins and minerals

Much has been written about vitamins and health. Unfortunately, some of what has been written is quite misleading. Eating large quantities of pure vitamins, for example, is not likely to do you much good. Water soluble vitamins, such as the B vitamins and vitamin C, are simply excreted if taken in excess of bodily needs. The body uses as much as it wants and throws out the rest. On the other hand, large doses of fat soluble vitamins, such as vitamin A and D, actually may do you harm. As the doses of these vitamins get higher and higher, they become toxic. A sufficiently high dose actually may act as a poison, and may even cause death.

Also, vitamins in pill form are refined food and lack all the associated nutrients of their natural state. Nutrients often work better in combination than alone, and nature usually can be relied upon to do a good job of putting foods together in the right form.

By all means, use vitamin supplements to be certain in some cases. Women often need vitamins with iron, for instance. Basically, however, we recommend that if you want to be sure of your vitamin C, don't pop pills. Try good, old-fashioned, juicy and delicious oranges.

3. Recording your present level of nutrition

The starting point for assuring good nutritional habits is to take an honest, accurate stock of your food intake. Then, this needs to be evaluated in terms of the basics of nutrition mentioned in the previous section. Weaknesses need to be noted so gradual changes can be made in your eating habits.

TABLE #6
FAT CHART

PERCENT FAT	0	10	20	30	40	50	60	70	80	90	100
Cheddar cheese	─────────────────────────										
Cheeseburger	────────────────────										
Cottage cheese	────────										
Chocolate chip cookie	───────────────										
Chicken without skin	───────										
Donut	─────────────										
Egg	─────────────────────										
Haddock (poached)	──										
French fries	─────────────										
Ice cream	────────────────										
Milk (whole)	───────────────										
Weiner	───────────────────────────										

Each gram of fat has nine calories in it.
Each gram of carbohydrates (starch and sugar) has four calories.
Therefore, for people watching calories, eyes should be focused on fats, not carbohydrates

91

The two charts on the following pages will help you with this personal assessment. On the first chart, record all foods and approximate amounts you eat for one week (days 1 to 7). Be sure to include snacks as well as alcoholic drinks. At the end of the week transfer the information to the evaluation chart which follows the record chart. The evaluation chart has boxes and triangles to indicate one serving of each food type. The number of boxes represent the ideal number of serving for an adult. If you fill in any triangle, you know you are consuming more than the daily recommended amount of food in that group. If you are a pregnant or nursing mother, an adolescent, or an extremely active person, those extra calories may be all right. Consult the Food Guide in Table #4 to check your allowable intake. Cut back if you are consuming too much in any one group. The circles represent empty calorie food.

The following list, based on the Food Guide, gives examples of servings that equal one unit (a box or triangle).

Breads and cereals

- 1 slice bread
- 125 - 250 mL (½ - 1 cup) cooked or ready-to-eat cereal
- 125 - 200 mL (½ - ¾ c) cooked rice, macaroni, spaghetti

Milk and milk products

- 250 mL (1 cup) milk, yogurt, or cottage cheese
- 45 g (1½ oz) cheddar or process cheese

Meat and alternates

- 60 - 90 g (2 - 3 oz.) cooked lean meat, poultry, liver, fish
- 60 mL (4 tbsp.) peanut butter
- 250 mL (1 cup) cooked dried peas, beans, or lentils
- 80 - 250 mL (⅓ - 1 cup) nuts or seeds

- 60 g (2 oz.) cheddar, process, or cottage cheese
- 2 eggs

Fruits and vegetables

- 125 mL (½ cup) vegetable or fruit
- 125 mL (½ cup) juice
- 1 medium potato, carrot, tomato, peach, apple, orange, or banana

Coffee and tea

- 1 cup

Alcohol

- 1 (12 oz.) beer
- 4 oz. table wine
- 3 oz. fortified wine
- 1 ½ oz. hard liquor

Empty calorie foods — See Table #7

After you complete the evaluation chart, note the excesses and deficiencies in your present food pattern. Write down one to five changes you plan to make in your food intake. It is useful to write down even minor changes. Your list might look like the one in Sample #9. Now make your list using the blank form provided on page 96.

4. Diet and weight control

These days, dieting must be the second-most talked about subject after the weather. And, given the bewildering variety of diets available and the speed with which they win or lose favor, it seems that dieting is no more predictable than weather forecasting.

At the risk of spoiling the mystique, the following simple, but difficult to carry out formula is offered. It has four common sense elements:

(a) Know your ideal weight

(b) Exercise to the point of obtaining physical fitness

(c) Eat well-balanced low-calorie foods

(d) Change your eating habits

EATING RECORD CHART

	DAY 1	DAY 2	DAY 3	DAY 4	DAY 5	DAY 6	DAY 7
BREAKFAST							
SNACKS AND DRINKS							
LUNCH							
SNACKS AND DRINKS							
SUPPER							
SNACKS AND DRINKS							

DIET EVALUATION CHART

	DAY 1	DAY 2	DAY 3	DAY 4	DAY 5	DAY 6	DAY 7	YOUR TOTAL	IDEAL (ADULT)
1. Breads and cereals	□□□□□▽ ▽▽▽▽▽	□□□□□▽ ▽▽▽▽▽	□□□□□▽ ▽▽▽▽▽	□□□□□▽ ▽▽▽▽▽	□□□□□▽ ▽▽▽▽▽	□□□□□▽ ▽▽▽▽▽	□□□□□▽ ▽▽▽▽▽		28-35 or more
2. Milk and milk products	□□▽▽▽▽ ▽	□□▽▽▽▽ ▽	□□▽▽▽▽ ▽	□□▽▽▽▽ ▽	□□▽▽▽▽ ▽	□□▽▽▽▽ ▽	□□▽▽▽▽ ▽		14 or more
3. Meat and alternates	□□▽▽▽▽ □	□□▽▽▽▽ □	□□▽▽▽▽ □	□□▽▽▽▽ □	□□▽▽▽▽ □	□□▽▽▽▽ □	□□▽▽▽▽ □		14 or more
4. Fruits/vegetables	□□□□□▽ ▽▽▽▽▽	□□□□□▽ ▽▽▽▽▽	□□□□□▽ ▽▽▽▽▽	□□□□□▽ ▽▽▽▽▽	□□□□□▽ ▽▽▽▽▽	□□□□□▽ ▽▽▽▽▽	□□□□□▽ ▽▽▽▽▽		28-35 or more
5. Coffee and tea (1 cup)	○○○○○○ ○○○○○○	○○○○○○ ○○○○○○	○○○○○○ ○○○○○○	○○○○○ ○○○○○○	○○○○○ ○○○○○○	○○○○○ ○○○○○	○○○○○ ○○○○○		21 or less
6. Alcohol	○○○○○○ ○○○○○○	○○○○○○ ○○○○○○	○○○○○○ ○○○○○○	○○○○○ ○○○○○○	○○○○○ ○○○○○	○○○○○ ○○○○○	○○○○○ ○○○○○		12 or less
7. Empty calorie food	○○○○○○ ○○○○○○	○○○○○○ ○○○○○○	○○○○○○ ○○○○○○	○○○○○ ○○○○○○	○○○○○ ○○○○○○	○○○○○ ○○○○○	○○○○○ ○○○○○		21 or less

(a) Know your ideal weight

For most people, the weight they achieve when they stop growing as teenagers is their ideal weight. Thus, if you were 125 pounds (57 kg) in your late teens, you should be within 10 pounds (4.5 kg) of that at age 40. Since most people become less active as they grow older, therefore carrying less weight as muscle, the 10 pound variation should be below, rather than above, the ideal mark.

Height and weight charts can be helpful, but they provide only a rough guide. If you are within 10 pounds (4.5 kg) of your ideal weight and are physically fit, you are likely as close to your ideal weight as you need to be for health reasons. If you are not physically fit, you may have very little muscle and still have too much fat, even though you may be close to your ideal. If you do not know your ideal weight, ask your doctor to help you establish it.

Here is a general guide to follow:

Males:

106 pounds + 6 pounds for each inch over 5 feet

Example: five feet, eight inches = 106 + 48 = 154 pounds

Females:

100 pounds + 5 pounds for each inch over 5 feet

Example: five feet, two inches = 100 + 10 = 110 pounds

For a small frame, subtract 10%; for a large frame, add 10%.

TABLE #7
EMPTY CALORIE FOOD CHART

Empty calorie food	Portion	Calories	Fat (tsp.)	Sugar (tsp.)	# of empty cal. units
Brownie	3" x 1" x 7/8"	95	1⅓	⅔	2
Butter	pat	36	1	0	1
Cake, iced	2" x 2"	203	2	4	6
Chocolate bar	40 g	216	2	5½	7½
Cereal, sugar coated	1 cup	109	0	3	3
Coffee creamer	1 tsp.	32	⅔	0	⅔
Donut	one	269	3½	3	6½
French fries	10	214	2	0	2
Fruit drink	1 cup	132	0	7½	7½
Gelatin dessert	½ cup	70	0	3	3
Jam, jelly, honey	1 tbsp.	54	0	3½	3½
Ice cream	½ cup	174	1	3½	4½
Milkshake	10 oz.	124	1	10	11
Oil	1 tbsp.	124	3	0	3
Pastry	one	269	3½	3	6½
Pie	3" wedge	302	2½	8	10½
Popcorn, oil, salt	1cup	59	½	0	½
Salad dressing, oil	1 tbsp.	66	1	0	1
Soft drink	10 oz.	138	0	9	9
Sugar	1 tsp.	15	0	1	1
Syrup	1 tbsp.	59	0	4	4
Sweet sauce	2 tbsp.	132	1	5	6

SAMPLE #9
DIET CHANGE LIST

1. Have one extra fruit a day — keep oranges, apples, papayas in the house.
2. Have cereal four times a week (instead of just coffee).
3. Decrease ice cream, chocolate bars, and soft drinks by 50%.
4. Buy yogurt and cottage cheese (to make up for no milk drinking).
5. Shop at the fish market each week.

DIET CHANGE FORM

1._____

_____

2._____

_____

3._____

_____

4._____

_____

5._____

_____

(b) Exercise and weight loss

As was mentioned in the exercise section, becoming aerobically fit increases the efficiency of your body. Your metabolism changes, you burn more fat, and you become thinner. It is strongly recommended that exercise be an integral part of any weight loss program.

To lose 1 pound (0.45 kg) you must burn 3,500 calories.

(c) Eat well-balanced lower calorie foods

We suggest that you forget about dieting as such. Rather, evaluate your nutritional intake. Find the high calorie foods and cut the intake down by a third or half. Add some lower calorie foods or eat more of the ones you enjoy. Plan a style of eating that fits your social and cultural situation, and stay with it for the rest of your life. Make sure that it is balanced and gives you your daily requirements. You will then be assured of weight loss that is slow, gradual, healthy, and permanent.

(d) Change your eating habits

North American eating habits are a major contributor to obesity. Here is a sampling of the hundreds of tips available to help you break poor eating habits —

- Shop so that only the very best food is in the house. If empty calorie food is not at home, you are not likely to eat it. As parents and adults, you can control the environment for you and your children. Keep empty calorie foods out of the house and out of schools. Children can indulge occasionally, but should not do so as a daily routine.

- When you snack, put the snack packet away before you eat. For example, take two cookies from the packet, put the packet away, then eat. Often we eat only because the food is in front of us, out of habit.

- At meal time, don't bring serving dishes to the table. If someone wants seconds, let that person to go the kitchen for more.

- Use smaller dinner plates and serve yourself smaller portions.

- Eat more slowly, put down your fork, chew each mouthful, and swallow it before having another forkful.

- Buy less food. Buy one donut, not a dozen. Buy only the very best chocolates or candy; the cost will tend to ration them. We do not advise eating candy or donuts but we realize the difficulty in giving them up completely, so offer this suggestion for cutting down when possible.

- Buy half bottles of expensive wine rather than whole bottles of cheaper varieties.

- Use a means of socializing other than dinner parties. Much excessive eating takes place on these occasions. Try eating alone first, then going out to a show with your friends.

- Take your time. All too often North Americans eat on the run. We wolf a sandwich at our desks, snatch a bowl of soup in the airport restaurant, gulp down dinner before a show, or bolt a hamburger on the way to a game. Fast food is now a vast industry, and grabbing a bite has grown from a colorful expression to a way of life. It is time to slow down. Eating on the run probably produces as much stress as two days without any food at all. You need periods of rest both before and after meals. If you sit down preoccupied and tense, your body may fail to produce the necessary digestive enzymes. You need a period of anticipation to literally get the juices flowing before you eat. Similarly, after a meal, you need to take time to let the digestive process work. Digestion takes energy. A great burst of activity after eating will inhibit the work of both the stomach and the small bowel.

Eating should be a pleasure, never a nuisance, a chore, or a piece of business to finish as quickly as possible. Make every meal an occasion. Look forward to it as a period of rest. Don't eat mechanically; instead, enjoy every mouthful.

c. HARMFUL HABITS TO RECONSIDER

- "Come in, have a cup of coffee!"
- "What can I offer you, gin, rum, rye?"
- "Ma, can I have a coke?"

The use of drugs is so much a part of our civilization, and so taken for granted, that many people are quite unaware that they are using drugs at all. A person who has six cups of coffee a day would probably be stunned if told that they are approaching the medical category of the drug abuser.

If the use of common drugs, such as caffeine, alcohol, and nicotine, were confined to celebrations and social occasions, there would be no objection to them. But this evil trio is now so widespread, and taken in such high daily dosages, that probably three quarters of the population are addicts of one sort or another.

The irony is that while these drugs are often taken to combat the effects of stress — for instance, a drink to "perk you up" — regular use creates more stress for the body than the drugs alleviate. The same is often true of some other types of drugs such as tranquilizers.

It may be hard to face the possibility that you are abusing something that has become a part of your daily life, particularly when everybody else is doing the same. However, you will do yourself an enormous favor if you start to cut down or cut out, and it is no exaggeration to say that you may add years to your life.

Before discussing specific habits in detail, record an estimate of your present consumption on the Consumption Chart on the following page. Try to be as accurate as you can, and don't judge yourself in advance.

1. Caffeine

Caffeine is the drug that gives coffee its stimulating properties. What is not so widely known is that caffeine is also found in tea, colas, and chocolate.

As a stimulant, caffeine increases the body's metabolic rate and heartbeat, activates certain centers in the brain, and causes release of free fatty acids.

A cup of coffee two or three times a day for pleasure after meals won't harm you, but when you start to use it as a stimulant, trouble can occur. For instance, if you are tired and drink coffee to keep going, you may well feel better for awhile, but the caffeine is merely covering up the fact that your body needs rest. You are actually causing yourself undue stress. Pushed to an extreme, this cycle can increase your susceptibility to disease. Caffeine also inhibits your ability to relax, and it is well-known for its power to disturb sleep. Large amounts of caffeine are a hazard for pregnant women and have been linked to developmental defects in newborn babies. Expectant mothers should regard it as a dangerous drug and should avoid it as much as possible.

Children often drink far too much caffeine. Ideally, their consumption should not exceed half a bottle of cola (six ounces) in one day. They should not be given cola and chocolate bars together. A high level of caffeine consumption may cause excitability, irritability, and behavioral problems which few people would even think to blame on cola and candy.

2. Nicotine

There is only one sensible thing to say about smoking: quit!

Nicotine is an extremely toxic substance. Two or three drops (30 mg) of the pure alkaloid on the tongue will kill an adult in minutes. A typical cigarette contains 15 to 20 mg of nicotine, although the actual amount reaching the blood varies considerably, depending on such things as the characteristics of the filter, the depth and frequency of inhalation, and the length of the butt.

The long-term ill effects of smoking consist mainly of damage to the lungs and cardiovascular system. Smoking is believed to be the single most important factor in the development of lung cancer, and is also associated with cancers of the mouth and the respiratory tract and cancer of the bladder. Many respiratory diseases, notably bronchitis and emphysema, are much more likely to occur in smokers than in nonsmokers.

Smokers are also much more likely to have heart attacks, strokes, and circulatory ailments. They are more likely than nonsmokers to suffer stomach ulcers, or to have ulcers that heal slowly; skin wounds may heal less quickly in smokers.

Smoking women tend to have smaller babies, many more premature births, and a greater occurrence of miscarriages and

CONSUMPTION CHART

ITEM	QUANTITY PER DAY						
	Mon.	Tues.	Wed.	Thur.	Fri.	Sat.	Sun.
Coffee (cups)							
Tea (cups							
Chocolate drinks (cups)							
Chocolate bars (bars)							
Cola (12 oz. bottle)							
Beer (12 oz. bottle)							
Wine (4 oz. glass)							
Hard liquor (1½ oz.)							
Tranquilizers (tablets)							
Sleeping pills (tablets)							
Barbiturates (tablets)							
Amphetamines (tablets)							
Marijuana (joint)							
Cigarette, pipe, cigar (each)							
Other drugs							
TOTALS							

stillbirths. There is also evidence of impairment in the mental and physical development of the children of smoking mothers. Women smokers tend to reach menopause at an earlier age, and women smokers using oral contraceptives appear to be especially likely to suffer heart disease.

Many smokers claim that cigarette smoking is relaxing. While that may be true for some, the effect is short-lived. Within a few seconds the nicotine enters the blood where it stimulates heart rate, blood pressure, and respiration, and drops the temperature of the skin. In stressful situations, smoking a cigarette actually imposes higher stress levels on the body.

There are many self-help books and plans available to those who would like to stop smoking. If you are now a smoker and would like to quit, your physician will be able to give you advice or refer you to a smoking cessation clinic.

Finally, consider the social aspects of smoking as well. Smoking makes rooms, offices, and restaurants extremely unpleasant for other people. It also gives the smoker's breath a bad smell. So, for our sake as well as yours, we ask you again: please quit.

3. Alcohol

It is not generally recognized that alcohol use increases the risk of contracting a wide range of diseases, and that this risk increases with the amount consumed. If drinking is combined with smoking, the risks are even greater.

Cirrhosis of the liver is the most obvious alcohol-related disease. People who drink 20 or more bottles of beer a week, or 30 or more ounces of spirits are putting themselves in considerable danger of developing cirrhosis. General population death rates are also higher for drinkers at this level of consumption, particularly from heart disease, cancers of the lung, throat and mouth, pneumonia, accidents, and

suicide. Alcohol also increases the body's use of B vitamins, and may create a chronic deficiency of these essential nutrients, which in turn increases the risk of disease.

Another problem with alcohol is that people often have a drink to help themselves over a crisis, through a difficult time, or to help themselves unwind. More often than not, though, the drink merely covers up the stress rather than relieving it, and may contribute to serious chronic stress by hiding the body's needs.

In addition, combining alcohol with antihistamines (cold and allergy remedies), marijuana, tranquilizers, or barbiturates and other sleeping pills can be fatal. Alcohol can intensify the effects of these drugs, and vice versa. Many accidental deaths have been attributed to combinations of alcohol and other drugs.

As well, expectant mothers should strictly avoid alcohol for the fetus may develop congenital problems or brain damage if consumption is excessive.

The relatively low level of drinking at which dependence can begin is another factor that is not generally understood. For example, if you have three drinks a day, you probably would be offended if someone suggested you were a borderline alcoholic. But if those three drinks become a fixed routine, tolerance develops and the alcohol begins to have less effect. Over the years, the three drinks tend to get bigger in size, then more in number, until the moderate drinker has, almost without awareness, become a heavy drinker.

You might like to test yourself over a period of two or three weeks. First give up all alcoholic beverages for at least a week. How much do you miss them? Do you catch yourself saying, "Boy, I could sure use a drink!" Through the second week, allow yourself one drink a day. Do you look forward to it? In the third week just drink when you feel like it and see how quickly three drinks becomes your norm again. You may well be surprised at some of your reactions to this test.

We suggest a limit of 10 to 12 drinks per week. A drink is defined as a bottle of beer, one and a half ounces of hard liquor, or four ounces of wine. There has been some controversy over the benefits of alcohol, and certain researchers suggest that up to two drinks a day might actually protect us against some diseases such as heart attack. More than three drinks a day, though, definitely increases the danger of strokes, cirrhosis, and alcoholism.

Finally, if you drink, don't drive. Never. If you drink while away from home, take a taxi home. The cost is nothing compared to the risk of killing yourself or others.

4. Marijuana

Most users of marijuana (cannabis) describe its effects as euphoric. However, it has been found to act as a depressant over the long term.

High doses of marijuana over a longer period of time may lead to loss of energy and drive, slow and confused thinking, impaired memory, and lack of interest in any planned activity. Short-term effects include impairment of memory, logic, and the ability to perform complex tasks. Perception of sound, color, distance, and time are usually distorted. These effects make it extremely dangerous to drive a car while under the influence of marijuana.

Marijuana has been associated with increased incidence of chronic bronchitis and bronchospasm, and has also been associated with insomnia. The tar content of marijuana, when smoked, is at least 50% higher than that of tobacco. Heavy cannabis users, therefore, run an added risk of lung cancer, chronic bronchitis, and other lung diseases.

In most communities it is illegal to possess, sell, or grow marijuana. If you are caught, the stress incurred may not be worth the benefits sought. A wise approach would be that if you wish to smoke marijuana, do so very occasionally. If you find that you are using it frequently, you might wish to explore your motives.

5. Tranquilizers

Tranquilizers such as Librium and Valium are some of the most commonly prescribed today. They can be a valuable medication when used for short periods, but for many people they have become a way of life.

The problems caused by tranquilizers are twofold. First, the body easily develops a tolerance to these drugs and after 10 to 14 weeks it often becomes necessary to increase the dose in order to maintain the effect. Second, clincial evidence has shown that dependence on tranquilizers develops even at prescribed doses. After four to six months of use, a patient may experience physical withdrawal symptoms if intake is stopped abruptly.

Often, people continue taking tranquilizers on a long-term basis because they cannot or do not wish to face everyday life. Their sedated state helps avoid thinking about their problems. The futility of this course of action is indicated by the fact that tranquilizers are the most commonly used medication in cases of drug overdose, and their abuse is the leading factor associated with suicide attempts in North America.

Concern is being expressed about the use of tranquilizers by women during pregnancy and breast-feeding. Use of tranquilizers by an expectant mother may lead to dependence in the newborn baby.

An obvious problem is that tranquilizers can make you very drowsy. If you are taking such drugs, you should avoid driving or operating machinery.

In general, tranquilizers should only be used during an acute crisis. As soon as the crisis has passed, other methods of managing stress should be sought. The same philosophy applies to the use of stimulants, barbiturates, and sleeping pills.

6. Changing harmful habits

While the habits and customs we have been discussing are common, and for the most part, socially acceptable, you may, after consideration, decide to break some of them. There are a number of good books on the subject of changing habits or modifying your behavior. Some of these are listed at the end of this chapter.

If you wish to proceed right away, we suggest the following steps:

(a) Record your current intake or level of consumption for those habits you are interested in changing.

(b) Look for patterns or reasons that might account for your current behavior.

(c) Determine alternative methods for meeting the urges you habitually satisfy with socially acceptable drugs, and put these alternatives into effect. For instance, if you are used to drinking six cups of coffee at the office and decide to cut it down to two, you may choose to bring your own packages of herbal tea or coffee substitutes so that you can continue to enjoy a hot drink whenever you like. All you have to overcome is the slight inconvenience of making something different.

(d) Monitor and record your progress in a special booklet or diary. Start your program by making up this booklet to suit your unique purposes.

(e) Make sure that you solve any problems that come up while you are getting used to your alternatives. Otherwise you may find the new problems driving you back to your old habits.

(f) Continue to record your progress over a long period of time. Do not accept relapse as final.

(g) Reward yourself for your efforts — but not with chocolate! For example, treat yourself to a vacation after six months of not smoking.

(h) Look for suitable social support for reinforcement. For example, if all your friends are heavy smokers and drinkers, you may choose temporarily to limit your contact with them and join a group of joggers and exercisers who may also be giving up smoking or drinking.

Remember — no artificial stimulant or depressant is good for you. Using such a substance will only increase stress, while appearing to lessen it.

d. BUILDING SUPPORTIVE RELATIONSHIPS

Common experience and medical evidence show that the impact of stress in our lives is influenced by the strength and number of our social relationships. These relationships support us in times of crisis, provide us with feedback about our behavior, and give us access to emotional and spiritual fuel.

Recent research shows that death rates are lower for people with strong social relationships than for those who live more isolated lives. We all have different types of relationships. Those that have a positive and protective effect on our health are, in decreasing order of impact, spouse, other family, friends, religious group affiliations, and community organizations.

Research also has demonstated that marital status is related to rates of disease. For some diseases, rates are five to seven times greater for people who are divorced, separated, or widowed, than they are for those who are married.

There is some evidence that even pets provide a buffer against disease. A meeting of the American Heart Association reported that post-heart attack patients who owned pets were more likely to recover from their heart attacks than patients who did not. The pets in the study included dogs, cats, birds, gerbils, and iguanas.

Other studies have shown that pregnant women with close social connections have less difficulty during pregnancy and suffer fewer birth complications than women who lack such support. Both pregnancy and delivery are facilitated by warm and stable relationships. The recent return to more natural forms of birth and attempts to build a greater amount of social support into hospital settings, like encouraging husbands to take part in the delivery, are examples of how the stress of childbirth can be reduced.

Everyone needs a variety of social supports and you should make a deliberate effort to build them into your life. Some you can provide yourself; some provided by other people. You sho however, be aware of other peopl tolerances. You can seldom expect receive all your support from one person or one group of people. Such an expectation often leads to disappointment, anger, even depression.

1. Review your support network

A full support network involves a number of different people and a number of different ways of relating to them. These people may be real or fictional, living or dead. Fill out the questionnaire below to help review your personal support network. Check the box to the left of each source of support that applies to you. If you check a box, rate your level of satisfaction

PERSONAL SUPPORT NETWORK EVALUATION

KIND OF SUPPORTER	LEVEL OF SATISFACTION Low = 1 Medium = 2 High = 3
☐ Lover or spouse	
☐ Close friend	
☐ Parent	
☐ Brother or sister	
☐ Other relatives	
☐ People with common interests	
☐ Work associate	
☐ Helper in general	
☐ Counselor or mentor	
☐ Financial advisor	
☐ Person who energizes you	
☐ Person who challenges you	
☐ Person who respects you	
☐ Person who approves of you	
☐ Person who evaluates you	
☐ Pet (dog, cat, etc.)	
Total boxes:	Total score:

with that source of support by using the scale in the right-hand column.

2. Scoring and analysis

Your support system score has two parts. First, the range score tells you about the breadth or quantity of your support system. Compute this score simply by counting the number of boxes checked in the left-hand column.

If you total 0 to 4, you have a very narrow support system and are very vulnerable to change. A score of 5 to 8 shows a narrow system, but okay if spread over a variety of resources. A score of 9 to 12 is getting broader and is probably quite strong. A score of 13 to 16 is a very broad system and a good stress buffer if it is spread across a variety of resources.

Next, the satisfaction score reflects your average satisfaction level with the relationships you have, that is, their quality.

It is computed as follows:

$$\text{Satisfaction score} = \frac{\text{Total of satisfaction ratings score}}{\text{Range score (total number of boxes checked)}} \times 100 = \boxed{}$$

For example, if the sum of your satisfaction ratings is 18 and your range score is 8, then your satisfaction score is:

$$\frac{18}{8} \times 100 = 225$$

Scores may be interpreted as follows:

0-149	Low satisfaction level
150-249	Medium satisfaction level
250-300	High satisfaction level

Now consider the issues regarding your support system that are outlined in the Support Systems worksheet.

Remember, both the quantity and quality of relationships are important.

e. REST

Most people are aware of the need for rest. Less well-known is that obtaining proper rest is an essential part of stress management. You will be better able to handle a crisis, as well as the routine stresses and strains of daily life, if you rest periodically during the day and get a good night's sleep.

1. Leisure

Occasional breaks from your regular work and activities are very important. While you may think that this is obvious advice, ask yourself the question, "Do you practice it?"

Many people become so wrapped up in their daily activities that they never allow themselves so much as a five-minute pause from dawn to dusk. Indeed, some actually take pride in their workaholism.

The brain tires as much as the body, and while, by superhuman efforts, you may be super-productive, the quality of your output would probably improve if you did "take five" along with everyone else; go camping on the weekends, and look forward to some carefree weeks in a different place at least once a year.

It is true that North Americans are tending toward an over-abundance of leisure, but this should not obscure the fact that all of us need ample time to rest, to relax, to recuperate, and to refresh ourselves from our daily tasks. Some of the techniques described in chapters 2 to 6 are excellent tools for this type of rest.

2. Sleep

It is ironic that while we spend a great deal of our lives asleep, sleep itself is a subject about which relatively little is known. Before reading on, do the sleep evaluation worksheet on page 106.

Sleep is essential to health and normal functioning. Sleep deprivation experiments have shown that sleep-deprived individuals gradually become more and more incompetent, hallucinate, and exhibit bizarre behavior. Sleep deprivation is an integral part of brainwashing.

We also know that there seems to be a limit to sleep deprivation when the body eventually takes over — in self-defense, as it were — and the person goes to sleep in spite of everything. Even in the worst cases of insomnia, the sufferer eventually falls asleep.

It is also known that the metabolic rate is lower during sleep and that brain wave activity slows considerably. There is evidence that more body repair and growth take place during sleep than during waking hours.

Other studies have revealed that there are definite stages or levels of sleep. These consist of rapid eye movement, or REM, sleep, and Stages One, Two, Three, and Four.

The distinction among them is the depth or degree to which the sleeper is unconscious. REM sleep is the lightest; Stage Four the heaviest or deepest sleep. Strangely enough, the REM stage is the most important. Experiments have shown that people deprived of REM sleep feel less rested even though they may spend hours in the other stages.

The pattern of sleep is also not what you might expect. Instead of descending into a deep sleep and staying there, a person goes from one stage to another in a regular wave pattern repeated every one and a half to two hours. Thus, you will go from REM down to Stage Three or Four, then back to REM, then down again to Stage Three and so on. The depth, and the time spent at each depth, varies with age. Children tend to

SUPPORT SYSTEMS

1. The size of my present support system is_____

2. From my support network evaluation, the mix of my present support system is_____

_____

3. I use my support system for_____

_____

4. The main thing I'd like to change about my support system is_____

_____

5. Identify three people by name with whom you would like to improve your relationship or with whom you would like to establish one. Define the first action step for each.

_____

_____

_____

SLEEP EVALUATION

	POINTS
For each question below, recall your sleeping patterns over the past two weeks and choose the answer that best describes your experience. Then enter the corresponding point score in the points column. When you have answered all the questions, add up your score and refer to the key below.	

	POINTS

1. How long does it take you to get to sleep?
      — an hour or more   1 point
      — 40 to 60 minutes   2 points
      — 20 to 40 minutes   3 points
      — 20 minutes or less 4 points	

2. Once you are asleep, how much sleep do you get?
      — drastically less than I require   1 point
      — somewhat less than I require   2 points
      — more than I need   3 points
      — just the right amount 4 points	

3. When you wake up during the night, on how many nights during the last two weeks did you have difficulty falling back to sleep?
      — 6 or more nights   1 point
      — 3 to 5 nights   2 points
      — 1 to 2 nights   3 points
      — never 4 points	

4. On the average, how many times per night did you have this trouble?
      — 4 or more   1 point
      — 3 times   2 points
      — once or twice   3 points
      — zero 4 points	

5. During the past two weeks, what has been the general quality of your sleep?
      — fitful; I feel like I didn't sleep at all   1 point
      — moderate sleep disturbances   2 points
      — slight or occasional disturbances   4 points
      — sound sleep; I'm feeling well-rested 6 points	

6. What is your energy level during a typical day?
      — very drowsy; hard to stay awake   1 point
      — generally fairly tired   2 points
      — adequate energy for the day's tasks   4 points
      — highly energetic all day 6 points	

TOTAL	_____

24 - 28 points — Excellent sleeping pattern
21 - 23 points — Good; explore problem areas
19 - 20 points — Only fair; likely could improve
 0 - 19 points — Changes may be required. If you are able, bring the points up in the next few weeks with your doctor.

spend more time in Stages Three and Four; adults spend more time in Stages One and Two.

The cyclical pattern and varying depth of sleep account for the fact that it is quite normal to wake up at night. People in their twenties tend to wake up at least once a night; and in later years as many as four times. Often, the period of wakefulness is brief and may not even be recalled the next day. Even if full consciousness returns, it is important to be aware that waking is normal. Don't worry; you'll soon go back to sleep.

The amount of sleep needed depends on the individual. Some people manage well on five hours; others are miserable if they sleep less than eight. It is well-known that children require much more sleep than adults. If you find that you are needing more and more sleep, we suggest that you consult your doctor. You may have a physical problem or some emotional difficulty that you are repressing. Sleeplessness is indicative of excessive stress and can be a factor in psychological depression.

Some of the following guidelines for bedtime may help you have regular, sound sleep:

(a) Prior to going to bed, clear your mind. Review the things you have dealt with during the day and designate certain hours, days, or weeks in the future for unfinished business. Making a constructive plan helps you relax and keeps nagging, generalized worries at bay.

(b) Establish and follow a routine for going to bed. For example, wash up, prepare for bed, make sure that the cats are out, open the windows, and

lock the house. In other words, get settled for the night.

(c) Go to bed for sleep or for sex. Don't go to bed to watch TV, to read, or to think.

(d) Avoid any stimulants prior to going to bed. For caffeine, this period should be six to eight hours; for nicotine, it is two hours. Alcohol and marijuana will both disrupt sleep by causing you to wake up after a few hours of sleep.

(e) Have a drink of warm milk before bed.

(f) Make sure your bed is comfortable, the pillow is right, you have enough room to move, and that the room is quiet.

(g) When falling asleep, picture a pleasant thought in your mind, or a pleasant place where you'd like to be. This quietens the mind. Practicing relaxation exercises just before sleep can be helpful.

f. SUMMING UP

The purpose of this chapter has been to review the basic needs of good health and self-care for stress management.

In summing up, we return to the wisdom of considering your health in its total context. It is easier to develop this holistic approach to health when it springs from a system of beliefs on which you want to base your life. Then, what you do about nutrition, exercise, rest, social supports, and all aspects of well-being, will be compatible with your beliefs. If you believe in something, you are more likely to act on that belief. When your actions meet your health needs, it follows that you will be in a better position to deal with stress.

CHAPTER 7 READING LIST

Anderson, R. *Stretching*. Bolinas, California: Shelter Publications, 1980.

Bailey, C. *The Fit or Fat Target Diet*. Boston: Houghton Mifflin Co., 1984.

Coates, T.J. and Thoresen, C.E. *How to Sleep Better: A Drug-Free Program for Overcoming Insomnia*. New Jersey: Prentice-Hall, 1977.

Cooper, K.H. *The Aerobics Way*. New York: Bantam, 1978.

_____. *The Aerobics Program for Total Well-Being*. Bantam, 1983.

Health and Welfare Canada. *The Fit Kit: The Canadian Home Fitness Test*. Ottawa: Supply and Services Canada, 1975.

Milsum, J.H. *Health, Stress and Illness: A Systems Aproach*. New York: Prager, 1984.

Pomerleau, O.F. and Pomerleau, C.S. *Break the Smoking Habit: A Behavioral Program for Giving up Cigarettes*. East Hartford, Connecticut: Behavioral Medicine Press, 1984.

Satir, V.M. *Peoplemaking*. Palo Alto, California: Science and Behavior Books, 1972.

Shephard, Dr. R.J. and Dr. S.G. Thomas. *Fit After Fifty*. Vancouver: Self-Counsel Press, 1989.

Stewart, G. *Every Body's Fitness Book: A Simple Safe Sane Approach to Personal Fitness*. Garden City, New York: Doubleday, 1980.

Stewart, G. and Faulkner, B. *Bend and Stretch: Suppleness and Strength Exercises*. Victoria, British Columbia: 3S Fitness Group, 1979.

Underwood, R.D. and B.B. Underwood. *Wise and Healthy Living*. Vancouver: Self-Counsel Press, 1989.

APPENDIX
WORK SHEETS AND PROGRESS CHARTS

As you have worked through the different chapters and programs of this book, you have been asked to monitor your progress through a series of checklists and progress charts. Blank progress charts are included here for your convenience. If you need more charts than are provided here, you may copy them for your personal use only.

Instructions for completing these work sheets, and samples of how to fill them in are included in the text. The clearing work sheets and the time management logs are discussed in chapter 2. The progress charts and integrating relaxation progress charts are used in chapters 3, 4, and 5.

CLEARING WORKSHEET

PROBLEM, THOUGHT POSITIVE EVENT	C (Complete)	I (Incomplete)	PLAN

CLEARING WORKSHEET

PROBLEM, THOUGHT POSITIVE EVENT	C (Complete)	I (Incomplete)	PLAN

CLEARING WORKSHEET

PROBLEM, THOUGHT POSITIVE EVENT	C (Complete)	I (Incomplete)	PLAN

CLEARING WORKSHEET

PROBLEM, THOUGHT POSITIVE EVENT	C (Complete)	I (Incomplete)	PLAN

TIME MANAGEMENT DAILY LOG

TIME	ACTIVITY
MORNING	
AFTERNOON	
EVENING	

TIME	ACTIVITY
MORNING	
AFTERNOON	
EVENING	

TIME MANAGEMENT DAILY LOG

TIME	ACTIVITY
MORNING	
AFTERNOON	
EVENING	

TIME	ACTIVITY
MORNING	
AFTERNOON	
EVENING	

PROGRESS CHART

DATE	TIME OF DAY	LENGTH OF TIME	PHYSICAL STATE BEFORE	PHYSICAL STATE AFTER	MENTAL STATE BEFORE	MENTAL STATE AFTER	PULSE BEFORE	PULSE AFTER	HAND TEMP. BEFORE	HAND TEMP. AFTER	COMMENTS

PROGRESS CHART

DATE	TIME OF DAY	LENGTH OF TIME	PHYSICAL STATE		MENTAL STATE		PULSE		HAND TEMP.		COMMENTS
			BEFORE	AFTER	BEFORE	AFTER	BEFORE	AFTER	BEFORE	AFTER	

PROGRESS CHART

DATE	TIME OF DAY	LENGTH OF TIME	PHYSICAL STATE		MENTAL STATE		PULSE		HAND TEMP.		COMMENTS
			BEFORE	AFTER	BEFORE	AFTER	BEFORE	AFTER	BEFORE	AFTER	

PROGRESS CHART

DATE	TIME OF DAY	LENGTH OF TIME	PHYSICAL STATE		MENTAL STATE		PULSE		HAND TEMP.		COMMENTS
			BEFORE	AFTER	BEFORE	AFTER	BEFORE	AFTER	BEFORE	AFTER	

INTEGRATING RELAXATION PROGRESS CHART

SITUATIONS	QUICK RELAXATION ACHIEVED							
	WEEK 1	WEEK 2	WEEK 3	WEEK 4	WEEK 5	WEEK 6	WEEK 7	WEEK 8